BEFORE THE BYLINE

A Journalist's Roots

BEFORE THE BYLINE

A Journalist's Roots

DON WYCLIFF

Copyright © 2025 Don Wycliff

All rights reserved. No part of this book may be reproduced in any form or by any means without written permission from the publisher.

Published by Soulstir Books, a division of Soulstir LLC
12412 Bittersweet Commons Blvd W #365
Granger, Indiana 46530

soulstirbooks.com

Soulstir® and Soulstir Books™ are trademarks of Soulstir LLC.

Edited by David Parker Jr.
Cover and dust jacket design: Amanda Geno
Interior design: Peter Grupico

Hardcover ISBN: 979-8-9927331-2-9

For Matthew and Grant
So you will know how it happened

CONTENTS

Prologue	*1*
Chapter 1: The Kiss	*5*
Chapter 2: Native Soil	*23*
Chapter 3: Transplanting	*37*
Chapter 4: Ashland Days	*49*
Chapter 5: Race	*61*
Chapter 6: Summertime	*69*
Images from My Roots	*85*
Chapter 7: Westward Ho!	*93*
Chapter 8: Living a Mile High	*103*
Chapter 9: Banks of the Wabash	*111*
Chapter 10: To du Lac	*127*
Chapter 11: Best of Times	*141*
Chapter 12: Finding My Calling	*151*
Epilogue	*161*
Acknowledgments	*165*

BEFORE THE BYLINE DON WYCLIFF

PROLOGUE

On a raw early April morning in 1993, while on vacation with my family, I stopped our rented car at an intersection at the edge of a village in southwestern Ireland. We were headed east, making our way to Dublin on country roads. I was looking for a traffic sign that would point the way to the next little town. I glanced out the passenger-side window and scanned the landscape 180 degrees from left to right. No sign visible—and nobody on the streets.

So I turned back to the left and, suddenly, standing on the curb facing us where there had been no one seconds earlier, I saw a young girl. She was very round of face and dark of skin, obviously of African ancestry. She looked to be twelve, or maybe thirteen, and she was bundled up against the morning chill but nevertheless had a bright smile on her face. I don't know how long I looked at her before I realized I was staring, and wondering as I did so, "Where did *you* come from? How did *you* get here?"

Now, having reached old age, I find myself asking those same questions about my own life, during which I have so often turned up in places and circumstances I never expected to be—places where I felt, at least initially, as out of place as that little black girl seemed to me in that windswept Irish country town. Places like the editorial board of

BEFORE THE BYLINE DON WYCLIFF

The New York Times, or the editorial page editorship of the Chicago Tribune, or the board of directors of the Robert R. McCormick Foundation.

Even today I find it easier to think of myself as the skinny, snaggle-toothed little black boy that I was in my earliest years, living in a nondescript house on a rural highway in an undistinguished little East Texas town, than as a "Distinguished Journalist in Residence," the title they gave me at Loyola University when I left the newspaper business for academia. But I haven't been that little black boy for more than seven decades.

And yet I still find myself asking the man who looks back at me from the mirror each morning: Where did *you* come from? How did *you* get here?

The short answer to the first question is that I came from another era and another America—from the era of overt racial segregation and the America that tolerated it.

To the second question, there is no short answer. It's a long story—of family, of faith, and of a nation that in the last half of the twentieth century seemed finally to have decided, in the words of Dr. Martin Luther King Jr., "to live out the true meaning of its creed: that all men are created equal ..." It's the story that I have tried to tell in the pages that follow.

I am one of the lucky generation of African-Americans who came along at just the right historical moment to reap the fruits of our ancestors' struggles for freedom and equality, and of what seemed until recently our nation's decision to put aside old ways and adopt new ones that would make for a fairer, more decent, more inclusive America.

I was born in 1946, the first year of the postwar baby boom and the best of all possible years for a black child to be born in the United States, up to that point. But it wasn't just my timing that was good; it was also my excellent choice of parents and forebears. Strivers all, they refused to be defeated by racism, rejection, and disadvantage.

And there was one other factor: my religion. Devout Catholics sprung from deep black Catholic roots, my parents took care to assure that my brothers and sisters and I—nine of us finally—were brought up in the church. That meant more than just taking us to Mass on Sunday and receiving the sacraments. It also meant making little pioneers of us, enrolling us in a white Catholic school at a time and in a place where black kids could not attend public schools with whites, and thereby ensuring that, when the doors of adult opportunity were opened, we would be equipped to walk through.

And those doors eventually were opened as the United States, under the moral pressure of the civil rights movement and the need to demonstrate to the world that it could practice what it preached to others, began to make good on the "promissory note" that Dr. King spoke of in his "I Have a Dream" speech.

So it was that in April 1965, there occurred the event that became the pivot, the axis upon which turned my life and biography. We were living then in Terre Haute, Indiana—my parents, my seven younger siblings and I. I was two months from high school graduation and still uncertain what I would do next. Then, as if through a series of miracles, I found myself admitted to one of the nation's premier institutions of higher learning, the University of Notre Dame, with a full scholarship. It was a life-changing development, not just for me but also for my entire family.

Just over four years after that, while I was in graduate school at the University of Chicago, I awoke on a December morning in my tiny South Side apartment, turned on my radio and heard the news of what the Chicago police said was a shootout on the city's West Side between them and members of the Illinois Black Panther Party. Two Panther leaders, Fred Hampton and Mark Clark, had been killed.

Assassinated, it turned out. Set up and assassinated.

BEFORE THE BYLINE DON WYCLIFF

The Chicago media immediately began to tear away the veil of lies and fabrications that the police attempted to hang around the killings. And it was the performance of the media on that story that led me to abandon academia and become a journalist. I was twenty-two then, and would go on to have a career of more than four decades in the news business.

But none of that could have happened if I hadn't had the upbringing and education that I had in those early years. Those are the years that I have tried to recount in the pages that follow.

CHAPTER 1
THE KISS

My life began on December 17, 1946, in the colored wing of Yettie Kersting Hospital in Liberty, Texas. Mother said she was one of the lucky ones in the ward that day: She had a bed to lie on, but some women had to sleep and nurse their babies on mattresses on the floor.

My first name was supposed to be Joel. In fact, if you go to the state of Texas' birth index, you'll find me identified that way: Joel Don Wycliff, born to Emily Broussard and Wilbert Wycliff. It was my paternal grandmother who urged them to change it to Noel because I was born so close to Christmas. So they did, and on my birth certificate I became Noel Don Wycliff. Why they started calling me by my middle name I don't know, but I suspect it was a gesture of defiance by Mother, who, not for the first time or the last, resented Grandma's interference.

My coming-to-be occurred at a highly consequential juncture in history. During the nine months I was *in utero*, the League of Nations officially went out of business and the new United Nations held its first meetings in New York; the World War II allies hanged ten convicted Nazi war criminals (an eleventh, Luftwaffe commander and Hitler deputy Hermann Goering, cheated the hangman by committing suicide the day before he was to be executed); India moved inexorably toward independence from Britain; the first bikinis went on sale in Paris; for-

BEFORE THE BYLINE DON WYCLIFF

mer heavyweight boxing champion Jack Johnson died; singers Leslie Gore, Linda Ronstadt and Cher, actress Candice Bergen, baseball star Reggie Jackson, businessman/buffoon/insurrectionist president Donald Trump, politicians George W. Bush and Bill Clinton, and actor Danny Glover were born; Mother Francis Xavier Cabrini became the first American to be canonized a saint; Notre Dame won college football's national championship; America conducted its first underwater nuclear bomb test; Dean Martin and Jerry Lewis staged their first show as a comedy team, and one of the last multiple lynchings in the United States happened in Georgia, when a mob of white men murdered two black couples near Moore's Ford Bridge.

Liberty, my birthplace, lies astride U.S. Highway 90, about halfway between Houston and Beaumont. But we lived—my parents, my older brother Francois, and I—in Dayton, Texas, about six miles west, six miles closer to Houston. Dayton and Liberty once had been parts of the same municipality, but at some point, "West Liberty" morphed into "Day's Town" and then into Dayton.

The town derived its name from an early white settler, Isaiah Cates Day, a Tennessean who moved to Texas in the 1840s and, according to the lore in the local black community, was as prolific a procreator as he was a farmer and a stock raiser, which he gave as his occupations in the 1860 and 1870 United States censuses.

The 1860 census showed Day to be a substantial slaveholder—the biggest in Liberty County—and the 1870 census made clear the effects of slavery's abolition on his financial fortunes. In 1860, when the Civil War started, Day owned real estate worth $25,000 and had a personal estate valued at $65,000. No doubt a substantial part of that personal estate consisted of the fifty-two humans listed as his property in the census's "slave schedule." By 1870, after the Civil War and the adoption of the 13th Amendment outlawing slavery, Day's real estate holdings had diminished to $5,000 and his personal estate to $2,500.

By the one account I have been able to find—that of a woman named Laura Cornish, who was a slave on his plantation at emancipation—Day was about as good a master as a slave could have hoped to have.

"We all calls him Papa Day 'cause he won't 'low none of his cullud folks to call him 'Master,'" Mrs. Cornish, by then an old woman, told an interviewer from the Works Progress Administration's Federal Writers Project in 1937. "He says we is born jes' as free as he is, only de other white folks won't tell us so, an' dat our souls is jes as white, an' de reason we is darker on de outside is 'cause we is sunburnt. I has hear of lots of good white folks an' and some bad white folks, but I don't reckon there was anyone what was as good to the cullud folks as he was."

Indeed, if "Papa Day" treated his slaves very like family. That may have been because some of them were. One of his slaves, Amanda Gibbs, gave birth to ten children, all of whom carried the surname "Day" and were, according to family lore, fathered by Isaiah Day. There is no documentation to establish this claim definitively, and the documentation that does exist is sketchy and far from conclusive. But presumably Amanda Gibbs, the best witness of all, knew who fathered her children.

The 1870 census—the first in which freed slaves were included on their own accounts as people, not property—lists a "Mandie Cribs," who at the time was forty-two years old and had five children of the same last name in her household. Mandie Cribs, it seems pretty clear, was "Amanda Gibbs," the white census enumerator having used her nickname (the same one used by Laura Cornish in her WPA narrative: "Aunt Mandy") and heard "Cribs" instead of "Gibbs." Just where the name Gibbs came from nobody seems to know. Significantly, "Mandie Cribs" and her five listed children all were marked down as mulatto, i.e., of mixed black-white parentage.

Exactly where Mandie Cribs'/Amanda Gibbs' five *other* children were on census day 1870 isn't clear. But one thing *is* clear from family records and testimony: All ten children were always referred to by the surname "Day," not Gibbs or Cribs, as the census enumerator recorded it.

The youngest child in that 1870 census listing, two-year-old "Lit"—her given name was Leana—grew up, was married twice and gave birth to two daughters and two sons. The second of her daughters, Ida Belle Brown, was my paternal grandmother, the one who insisted I be named "Noel." Ida's only child, a boy named Wilbert, was my father.

* * *

Wilbert—"Daddy" to me and my siblings—was twenty-eight when I was born, and not quite a year out of the United States Army, where he had spent fifteen months with the all-black 92nd Division—the Buffalo division—in Italy during World War II. He came home in January 1946 with three Bronze Stars and a first lieutenant's bars. And he quickly discovered that if war had been hell, peace as a black man in the American South was, well, hellish—even if that black man had helped save the world from fascist tyranny.

On my birth certificate, Daddy's occupation was recorded as "Blacksmith." Truth is, he was sharing a workplace and a diminishing amount of available work with his father, my grandfather, Socrates "Sprig" Wycliff, a second-generation blacksmith himself. Even as early as 1946, the trade of blacksmithing was on its way to the dustbin of history. There was just enough life left in it that I would be able, as a teenager in the early 1960s, to spend summers working with Grandpa in his shop and earn enough money to pay my Catholic high school tuition.

Mother—Emily Ann Broussard—and Daddy were married on June 2, 1942, in a Catholic ceremony at St. Patrick's Church in Bisbee,

Arizona. Mother was a devout Catholic, raised in a household where, for reasons of finances and distance, going to Mass on Sunday was not always possible, but getting each new baby baptized was a priority. "When babies were born and had to be baptized," Mother said, "Mama would pay a neighbor to take her to Ames to get the baby baptized."

Ames, Texas, is lately best known as the town where Darren Walker, president of the Ford Foundation, grew up. But for most of its existence, tiny Ames (population 1,240) has been better known as the fountainhead of a black Catholic Creole community encompassing half a dozen small towns and settlements in the Liberty area, including Dayton. Served through most of its existence by Irish-American Catholic priests of the Society of St. Joseph—the Josephites—Our Mother of Mercy parish in Ames was the anchor church of this community. It was created in the 1920s on the initiative of community members, led by my great-grandfather, Sylvester Wickliff, and a cousin, Terrance Trahan. They had migrated to the Liberty area in the 1890s from the region around Lafayette, Louisiana, bringing their strong Catholic faith with them.

Eventually, Our Mother of Mercy grew to include not just a church, but also a rectory, a convent and a grade school, which was staffed by black nuns, members of the New Orleans-based Sisters of the Holy Family. Mother attended Our Mother of Mercy school for three years, thanks to her aunt, Amanda Darby, who had become Sister Mary Ambrose in the Holy Family sisters.

Daddy, by contrast, was raised pretty much indifferent to religion. His father, Socrates, grew up in the Ames Catholic community but was divorced as a young man. That put a wedge between Socrates and the church. Daddy's mother, Ida, was Baptist. Daddy says he grew up going to whatever church was handy or, as often as not, to no church at all. However, respecting the Catholic Church and abiding by its requirements was part of the deal if he wanted to marry Emily Broussard, so Daddy took the deal.

BEFORE THE BYLINE DON WYCLIFF

They were married in Arizona because Daddy, twenty-three at the time, was in the Army, stationed at nearby Fort Huachuca, where he and the rest of the 92nd Division were preparing for deployment to the European theater of the Great War. Mother, two weeks shy of her twentieth birthday, had come out from Dayton on the train. When she returned home a few weeks later, she carried not only a new last name—Wycliff—but also, *in utero*, the couple's first child, Francois, who would be born on March 24, 1943.

* * *

Mother was the second oldest of ten children. Her parents—Napoleon "Paul" Broussard and Ezildia Darby Broussard—were refugees from Louisiana, from the region around Lafayette known as Acadiana—Cajun country—for the French speakers who settled there after being expelled from Canada's maritime provinces after the French and Indian War ended in 1763.

In slavery times, Louisiana had been one of the places slaves referred to when they spoke fearfully of being "sold down the river." So Acadiana also was home to a large population of black people, many of whom emigrated to East Texas in the late 1800s and the early 1900s. For the most part, they moved in search of economic opportunity, but in many cases, they literally fled ahead of lynch mobs.

Paul Broussard—"Papa," Mother called him, and we children followed suit—had come to Dayton in 1919, following in the footsteps of an older stepbrother. Both had somehow run afoul of white folks in Louisiana and sought refuge in East Texas.

Mother said Papa had spent a year in jail in Louisiana for carrying a concealed weapon. He also reportedly incurred white wrath by opening a small business where he cleaned, pressed and tailored men's clothes. This apparently stirred resentment among whites, who accused him of wanting to "make his living sitting down like a white man."

For most black folks in that part of Louisiana, making a living meant laboring long hours in sugar cane fields. It was grueling and dangerous work, all for little or no money. Compared to what they faced in Louisiana, even segregated East Texas seemed progressive. And so they came in large numbers to towns and settlements like Dayton, Liberty, Raywood and Ames.

In December 1919, Papa "slipped back" into Louisiana to marry Ezildia Darby, the daughter of Simon Darby and Mella Provost Darby of Youngsville. Immediately after their marriage on December 3, the newlyweds lit out for Dayton, where they bought a lot at the corner of Austin Street and Cleveland Road on the north end of town, built a small house and set about raising a family.

Papa was thirty-nine then, and Ezildia twenty-five. The neighborhood where they lived was called the French Settlement, because it was heavily populated with people like them: French-speaking black folks from Louisiana, most of them Catholic.

I have no personal memory of Ezildia—"Mama"—who died at age fifty-five in 1950, just after I had turned three. The few photographs of her that exist show a tall, slender, dark-skinned woman. Mother said she was an outstanding cook. When she left Louisiana after her marriage, the white family for which she had worked reportedly lamented the loss of "the best cook in the area."

"Zilda," as she was known to her friends, was immensely popular in the French Settlement and, as a result, the Broussard house was a favored gathering spot in the community. The neighborhood women would meet on Zilda's front porch to drink strong coffee, brewed and served by her daughters, and share gossip, while their children played in the yard.

I *do* remember Papa. He was tall, salt-and-pepper-haired and had skin the color of a polished pecan shell. In my memory, he would walk

BEFORE THE BYLINE DON WYCLIFF

down the road to our house every evening to eat dinner and listen to Gabriel Heatter deliver the news on the radio. I've since learned that Heatter was regarded as a voice of optimism, a man who always found the silver lining around any cloud. "There's good news tonight!" was his signature greeting. But at the time, his voice seemed to my child's ears too full of portentous quaver to be delivering good news. And Papa always seemed to me to walk away from the broadcast disturbed, not heartened, by what he had heard.

Nine of Papa's and Mama's children lived to adulthood. The youngest, a boy named Richard, died at about seven weeks of whooping cough. The eldest, Grant, died at age twenty-one in January 1942, after a life marked by severe illness and disability. Apparently, as a result of a fall from a tree when he was still in grade school, the right side of his body simply ceased to grow properly, Mother said.

Between Grant, the first-born, and Richard, the last, came four girls and four other boys. Mother was the oldest of all these, born June 15, 1922.

When Papa and Mama first settled in Dayton, he worked for the railroad—which one I'm not certain. As their family grew—and as the couple prospered during the 1920s—Papa added to their house. He was, Mother said, a "jack of all trades"—carpenter, field worker, yard man, anything that would bring in a buck. But his desire to have his own business, to be his own boss, had not been extinguished by his experience in Louisiana.

About 1927, he built another small structure next to his house and opened a barber shop and a shop where he would clean and press clothes and order men's suits. On weekends, from a different side of the same building, he and Ezildia sold ham sandwiches, cold drinks, gum, candies, homemade ice cream and kerosene for lamps to people from the neighborhood.

"They did real well until the Depression hit in the early 1930s,"

Mother said. "When the bottom fell out of everything, there was no work other than yard work and field work. A whole day's work for one dollar—picking cotton, potatoes, peas, and so forth."

For her part, Mama took in washing and ironing for white folks, tasks with which her daughters helped. "We had no electricity," Mother said. "We heated our irons on wood-burning stoves. We had to wipe them real good and clean before putting them on a white garment. Later on, when we got up in the world, we bought a furnace that we could put coal into to heat the irons."

The Depression seems to have done what racism and other obstacles could not: demoralize Paul Broussard. He was reduced to going out each day in search of work. If he was lucky, he found something and could bring home food for his family. Many times, he found nothing.

Mother described him as "a meek and mild person," although that hardly squares with the image of a man who acquired and carried a gun to defend himself against racial terrorists in Louisiana and who persisted for years in the determination to have his own business. What Papa seems to have become was a defeated person—defeated by the Depression, defeated by circumstances beyond his control.

In 1953, with his wife deceased and all but his youngest living son out of the nest, Papa decided to visit Seattle, where three of his children had moved in pursuit of jobs in the postwar economic boom. Ten months later, in July 1954, Papa died in a Seattle hospital after what a newspaper obit described as "a long illness."

* * *

Wilbert—"Daddy"—grew up thinking he was an only child, only to learn when he was at the threshold of adulthood that he had two half-brothers. They were products of a relationship between his father, Socrates, and a woman he lived with for several years during his footloose younger days.

"He told me he had gone to Galveston to work," Daddy said, describing how his father had disclosed this family secret to him, "and he cohabited with this woman who he thought to be a mamoo, a real light-skinned Creole woman. She was actually Italian. They had one son, Edward, and a couple years later another son, Raymond. Then one day they had an argument and she called him 'nigger' and told him her true identity."

A black man didn't need to be a Socrates to see the explosive potential in that kind of situation, so Grandpa quickly found his hat and the front door. He moved to Houston, leaving behind two sons who, as far as he knew, remained in Galveston and continued to carry his last name, but lived as white men.

Socrates went on to marry Ida in 1916 and to settle into a life of quiet domesticity, fathering another son, Wilbert, who was born in October 1918. Wilbert lived the life of a regular country boy until 1931, when he was 13. That's when Ida's older sister, Leana Day's oldest child, Willie, came home for a visit from Washington, DC, where she worked at the Treasury Department's Bureau of Engraving and Printing, helping produce the nation's currency.

During that visit, Daddy said, she "saw something in me that she thought Washington would help." It was decided that he would go to live with her and attend school in the nation's capital.

He was thirteen when he left for Washington in 1931, but so small that he was able to pass for twelve and ride the train for half-fare. The journey took three days and was itself a significant learning experience. "Mama tagged me like I was parcel post," he said. "I traveled in August in a wool suit, carrying an overcoat. I did fine until I got to Little Rock, where the cars were switched and whites and colored began riding in the same car. I was uncomfortable, having grown up in a totally segregated society."

He ended up staying in Washington three years, until the Depression made it financially impossible for Aunt Willie to continue to keep him. "Many, many years passed before I realized how blessed and valuable those three academic years were in my life," he said. "I don't know how a country boy from Texas could command so much respect and admiration. I was elected class president in the seventh, eighth and ninth grades at three different schools. I was not especially smart, but I studied hard, kept up with my work and had a normal social life."

Better schooling, albeit still segregated schooling, was only part of the benefit of living in Washington. The city itself was a classroom, and the times—it was the era of Franklin Roosevelt's New Deal—provided a rich curriculum. "The Capitol Rotunda was my playground," he said. "I would skate from 11th and G Streets N.E. to the Washington Monument, walk up to the observation deck. Visit the White House a couple of times a year. Go to the Bureau of Engraving and Printing in time to take the last sightseeing tour. Look down [from a catwalk] on Aunt Willie while she worked and then wait to go home with her after she got off from work.

"I was at Franklin Roosevelt's [1932] inauguration. I stepped on a woman's foot with my roller skates on. She was not a happy Democrat.

"I loved to go to the Dunbar Theater to see the cowboy shows. I would save my lunch money to go to the Howard Theater, the Lincoln Theater or the Booker T. Theater when a good show was on. The Howard always had a movie and a stage show. Duke Ellington, Jimmy Lunceford, Chick Webb, Cab Calloway and others were regular performers there ... I had a great appreciation for those places of entertainment because I didn't have to sit in the balcony—the 'buzzards' roost'—like back home in Dayton.

"I would go to the zoo quite often. I also went to the library regularly. I developed some culture and learned to appreciate some of the finer things of life ... Each Saturday, I had [violin] lessons at the Washington Conservatory of Music—I even played with the conservatory orchestra. I learned to touch-type in the ninth grade. I had a speed of about forty-five words per minute. This was the key to my achievement in later life, especially in the Army and in college."

After three years, however, Wilbert's Washington idyll ended. As the Depression deepened and lengthened, Aunt Willie's hours at her government job were cut, and then cut again. Eventually, she found herself no longer able to keep her nephew, who had to return to Dayton.

* * *

By the time Daddy returned in 1934, Sprig, who previously had worked for others, had opened his own blacksmith shop in downtown Dayton. Ida, who had been a public school teacher before Wilbert's birth, had gone back to teaching.

"Our family was always considered well-off," Wilbert said. "People thought we had more than we had. In the '30s, there were times when Daddy didn't make enough at the shop to bring home sugar or flour or something. But we always had enough to eat. We farmed. We raised livestock and chickens and such. And we had good credit."

Wilbert was in tenth grade when he returned to Dayton, and tenth grade was as far as one could go then at Colbert High School, the colored school. So after graduating from high school in Dayton, he went one more year to the black high school in Liberty and graduated there too. Then it was on to Prairie View A&M.

In those days of "separate but equal," Prairie View was the state's land-grant university for blacks. For an ambitious young black Texan, it was *the* place to go to college. Problem was, seventeen-year-old Wilbert wasn't very ambitious. Without regular adult guidance for the first time in his life, he behaved in college like an aimless teenager and compiled an academic record studded with Fs and Ds. By the spring of 1937, the end of his freshman year, he knew he would not be returning in the fall. The question was: What to do instead?

His Uncle Luther Wells, who operated a mortuary in Liberty, came to the rescue, arranging an apprenticeship for his nephew with a colleague in Galveston. That led Socrates to disclose to his youngest son the secret of his older brothers.

Daddy completed the mortician's apprenticeship and, after he turned nineteen, took the state exam and became a licensed funeral director. Grandma and Grandpa then mortgaged their cattle to get him the $300 tuition for embalming school. He completed the course and passed the state test. But, showing the same immaturity he displayed at Prairie View, he lost the receipt showing he had paid his tuition and was denied the embalmer's license.

So Daddy began "knocking around," moving from one odd job to another. In 1940, at his mother's urging, he returned to Dayton, where he drove a school bus and worked part-time at the QP, a downtown grocery store.

* * *

Meanwhile, Emily was in her last year at Colbert High where she would graduate as class valedictorian in May 1941. At the time, the Dayton school district provided bus transportation for black elementary school children, but not for high schoolers. High school students had to walk to school, and for Mother and others in the French Settlement, that meant a hike of at least three miles each way to Colbert High in Lowoods, the black neighborhood on the south end of town.

As if the walk weren't challenge enough, they faced taunts from white children riding buses to their separate but "more equal" school. When the buses went past, Mother said, the white kids would spit on them or hit them with switches they had brought aboard the bus.

One day Daddy, who was driving black elementary school students to Colbert, offered to let Mother ride the bus if she would kiss him. She thought on it, decided he was worth it and gave him a kiss. Thus began a relationship that lasted until death parted them in 2013, almost three-quarters of a century later.

Daddy was smitten, and when Christmas came around that year, he wanted to give Mother a gift. In the newspaper, he saw a jewelry store ad for a "dinner ring" for $9.50. He bought one, took it to Mother's house and gave it to her. Her mother, Ezildia, asked the young man, "Are you serious?" To which Daddy, without appreciating the full significance of what he was doing and saying, replied "Yes." And with that, Wilbert and Emily became engaged.

But there was no immediate trip to the altar. The following year, 1941, Daddy was drafted into the Army. The United States wasn't yet involved in the war that was raging in Europe and the Pacific, so draftees were expected only to go in, undergo a year of training and be released, to be recalled in the event they were needed. Daddy expected that after his training period was over, he would return to Dayton, and he and Mother would be married. But Pearl Harbor changed all that. After December 7, 1941, there were no quick exits from the armed forces. America was at war.

There was an obstacle on Mother's side as well. She had been working for years as a housekeeper and babysitter for a white couple, the Jamisons, both of whom were retired schoolteachers. Grace Jamison took a great liking to her and offered to pay for Mother to attend college. "She treated me like a daughter," Mother said.

Mrs. Jamison had hoped Emily would go to Prairie View, but instead she ended up going in autumn 1941 to Tillotson College, a small private institution in Austin. She stayed two weeks. She found herself underprepared academically and overwhelmed emotionally at being separated from her family.

Mother returned to Dayton, worked to repay Mrs. Jamison for the expenses of her brief college experience, and waited for Daddy's situation to clarify so they could be married.

Daddy, meanwhile, was finding his collegiate experience an advantage even though it had ended badly. Immediately after the Army induction ceremony in Houston, a commander asked whether any of the inductees had been to college. Daddy was the only one to raise his hand. He was promptly put in charge of getting the recruits and their paperwork to Fort Huachuca. Once there, someone asked whether anyone in his group knew how to type. Again, Daddy replied affirmatively. He became the company clerk, the Radar O'Reilly of his unit.

At Huachuca, Daddy and the other trainees were part of the all-black 93rd Division. Early in 1942, word got around that the division was ticketed for the Pacific theater of the war. When he heard about this, Daddy wrote to Mother and told her to forget about him, because the likelihood was that he wouldn't return alive. The Pacific, everyone said, was an abattoir. Mother lost hope.

Then, a few weeks later, there was a change of fortunes. Daddy was selected, along with fewer than 100 others, to remain behind at Huachuca and help revive the 92nd Division, the legendary black unit known during the Indian wars of the nineteenth century as the Buffalo Soldiers. They didn't know where the 92nd would ultimately be assigned, but they were pretty sure it wouldn't be the Pacific. Suddenly, Daddy was recalled to life—and Mother was called to a wedding.

She went out on the train. After she arrived, they made their way to Bisbee and found a Catholic church. The parish priest, Rev. James B. Davis, helped round up a couple of witnesses, and they tied the knot. They spent a few weeks together after the wedding. Then Mother returned to Dayton to await the birth of the baby they had conceived, and Daddy went back to soldiering, which was proving exactly what he needed to overcome his aimlessness.

A white commander urged him to apply for Officer Candidate

BEFORE THE BYLINE DON WYCLIFF

School, which he did. He was selected and became a second lieutenant. He and the rest of the 92nd ended up in Italy during the last months of the war.

In January 1946, he returned home and, like so many World War II vets, began trying to build a life for himself, his bride and their family. Building a family was the easy part. Mother quickly became pregnant with their second child—me—and, not long after my birth, with their third, my sister Karen.

But on the occupational front, things weren't working out so well. Finding a job that would support a growing family proved a challenge. Blacksmithing wasn't going to pay the bills, Daddy realized, so he needed something else. Using his GI benefit, he enrolled at the new Texas State University for Negroes in Houston. He majored in Industrial Arts and finished his bachelor's degree in three years, graduating in August 1950. But still, decent employment eluded him.

At one point, he took a civil service exam for a job as a postal clerk and scored well on it. So well, in fact, that word got around Dayton. A wealthy old rice farmer for whom Mother's sister, my Aunt Cecilia, worked, remarked to her one day, "What's your brother-in-law trying to do, take a white man's job?"

In the fall of 1951, about a year after the arrival of baby number four, Christopher, Wilbert took a job teaching industrial arts at a high school in Orange, Texas, about fifty miles east of Dayton. At the insistence of the local school authorities, he moved his family to Orange. We didn't stay long.

Mother hated the place with a passion. One night, she fell ill, and Daddy piled her and all the kids into the car and drove us back to Dayton, where we remained. From then on, he commuted to and from Orange, renting a room in a family's home and coming to Dayton once during the week and on weekends. It was an arrangement that neither he nor Mother liked.

On top of that, he chafed at having to teach his classes with castoff tools and materials from the white schools in Orange and being unable, as a result, to do a job that met his own standards. So he was soon searching again for new work.

One day early in 1954, he saw on a bulletin board in the Dayton post office advertisements for two jobs with the federal government. He decided to apply for both and told himself that he would take the first that came through.

A few weeks later, he got a letter from the Federal Correctional Institution in Ashland, Kentucky, offering him a job as an instructor in the institution's education program. They wanted him as soon as possible.

Daddy wrote back, saying that his current job would not end until the end of the school year in June. Could they wait for him until then? Yes, they responded. And so it was decided.

Daddy drove home from Orange after the last day of school there, Friday, June 4. Mother helped him get packed and ready to depart. The next day, he boarded a train that got him to Ashland in time to report for work on Monday morning, June 7. He quickly decided the job was a keeper, and he and Mother began making plans to move the family.

For both of them, Ashland, Kentucky, represented deliverance. For Daddy, it was deliverance from the frustration of unfulfilling, dead-end jobs in East Texas. For Mother, it was deliverance from the stultifying small-town life of Dayton and the constant interference of her mother-in-law. "Ashland was the first time we could call our own shots," she said. Ashland was freedom.

BEFORE THE BYLINE DON WYCLIFF

CHAPTER 2
NATIVE SOIL

If leaving Dayton was deliverance for Mother and Daddy, it was something else entirely for us children—certainly for Francois and me. With the exception of the brief, traumatizing few weeks that we lived in Orange, Texas, I had never known a home other than Dayton and our house on the Cleveland Highway. And from my seven-year-old's perspective, it was as good a home as anybody *could* want. Everyone and everything that mattered was there or within easy reach.

DON'S WORLD

If you walked out of our front yard to the highway and turned right (north), you would reach Papa's house after about a hundred yards, then Mr. Cap Kelly's house and his little store, then Uncle Sam Broussard's house, and then St. Joseph the Worker Catholic Church, our church, where we went every Sunday morning without fail and where Mother sang in the choir and Mr. Warren St. Julian sold ice cream cones after Mass.

Beyond the church was Diane Paul's house—Diane was my first-grade classmate, and I was supposed to marry her when we grew up. And beyond Diane's house was "The Overpass," where the highway

BEFORE THE BYLINE DON WYCLIFF

rose to cross over a set of railroad tracks. That overpass marked the limit of the world as I knew it in that direction. Beyond it lay ... I didn't know what, but at seven years old, who needed to know?

If you walked out of our yard and turned left, or south, you first passed the Mosleys' house—Robert, a white kid a couple of years older than I, his father Buddy and his grandmother—where they had a concrete pond in back in which they raised minnows to sell to fishermen. Then the Blue Gables, a honky-tonk for white folks that had blue neon lights around the edges of the roof and an illuminated sign that spelled out a mysterious word: "RENDEZVOUS." Then it was three or four miles to downtown Dayton. That's where all the stores were—Remke's and the QP for groceries, Mansfield's and McGinty's for drugs, Friedman's for hardware and dry goods. Mother shopped mainly at Remke's and Mansfield's, Grandpa used to say he "traded" at Friedman's, and all the adults in our family seemed to be on especially good terms with Sol and Esther Friedman, the owners.

Downtown was where the white schools were and where it seemed most of the white people lived. It was also where "the shop" was—Grandpa's big, red, corrugated tin-clad blacksmith shop, with its rear wall only a few yards away from the Southern Pacific Railroad tracks. Grandpa seemed to be the only colored person in Dayton with a business downtown—except for the very brief period when Mother opened a small café across the street from Grandpa's shop.

If you kept going south past downtown, you would end up in Lowoods, another black neighborhood. You'd pass Black Jack's tavern; Colbert Elementary and Colbert High, the colored schools. Then you'd find Pleasant Hill Baptist Church, Grandma's church, and a lot of houses and farm fields owned by colored people like Luke Walker, Gil Booth, Obie Jackson and Alfred Deaver. And finally, at the end of a dead-end road, amid a grove of pecan and walnut trees, you'd reach Grandma's and Grandpa's house and farm.

If you turned left when you got downtown, you'd be headed east on Highway 90 toward Liberty, Ames, and Beaumont. Aunt Stella, Grandpa's oldest sister, and her husband, Uncle Luther Wells, lived in Liberty and ran Wells Mortuary. Liberty was also where we would go occasionally to the Chevrolet dealership—Mearns Chevrolet—when the car needed fixing. There was a streetlight next to Mearns that attracted bugs of enormous size and number, and Mother used to tell the story of how I, a notorious daydreamer, one day mused, "Dem bugs sho was big in Yibitty" (I was about six years old before I could properly pronounce the letter L).

East of Liberty was Ames, where Grandpa had grown up and where his father, Sylvester ("Big Papa"), and three of his six siblings—Edward ("Timme"), Frances, and Magdalene ("Mac") still lived. By the time I came along, Big Papa was a shrunken little man who looked to me somewhat like the cartoon character Popeye and who seemed always to sit stiffly upright in a chair and speak in a barely audible voice when we went to visit him. But in his younger days, he had been a formidable character, builder of a successful business, owner of substantial real estate and pillar of the community in which he resided.

Uncle Timme, a tall, barrel-chested man, farmed and ran a Gulf gas station on Highway 90 and had a small factory where he made the sweetest, most delicious cane syrup in the world. He was the only person I knew who had fingers as big and thick as Grandpa's. Aunt Frances always seemed to me so pretty, but also terribly fragile. Aunt Mac seemed just the opposite: strong and feisty, robust and opinionated. I liked her.

Ames was where the black Catholic cemetery was, hidden way back in the woods, and where what seemed to me the biggest church in the world—Our Mother of Mercy—stood near the railroad tracks. I learned much later that Big Papa had donated half the land for the cemetery and considerable money for the construction of the church where he went to Mass every morning.

If you turned right when you got to downtown Dayton you would be headed west on U.S. 90 toward Houston, passing the liquor store just beyond the Liberty County line where Mother would go occasionally to buy a bottle of Mogen David wine for Papa, and the roadside curio shop where I once threw such a fit that Daddy bought me a little plaster cow that I coveted. (I promptly became terrified of it when we got it home and, to shut me up, someone hid it behind the piano in the living room. A short time later, Francois, unaware, shoved the piano to the wall and smashed the poor cow to bits.)

Houston was where Mother's sister Cecilia ("Nannan," we called her, because she was Francois' godmother and that was the Creole name for a godmother) lived in a neighborhood called Pleasantville with her husband, Uncle Robert Melonson, and our cousins Wanda, Wayne and Gary. They moved to Seattle not long after we left Dayton. Another of Mother's sisters, Aunt Georgia, and her husband, Uncle Dewey Collette, lived in another Houston neighborhood called Third Ward.

Houston was where Mother once drove with all of us children in the car to pick Daddy up when he was working at "the SP shop," the Southern Pacific Railroad roundhouse. I remember seeing the giant train engines and worrying that Daddy might get crushed by one of them, and being relieved when he finally walked out and got into the car and was alive and healthy.

And Houston was where every once in a very great while we would go downtown, where the tallest buildings in the world stood and where there was a five-and-dime store—Kress, I think—where they had a lunch counter and those tanks with red and yellow beverages in them, and I wished Mother would buy me some, but she never did.

Yes, everything that mattered was either in Dayton or close to it.

I could roll out of bed in the morning and, within a few minutes, meet up with my cousin Sam Brown and our friends Willie Kelly and "Hap" Thompson and half a dozen more. I remember one morning after a heavy rain, we went wading in the roadside drainage ditches and caught dozens of crawfish, which we carried back to my house and took turns crushing in the gravel driveway with Francois' bike and being surprised that the stuff that spurted out of them was yellow. Daddy came home that day and was furious—whether about the yellow mess all over the driveway or about our wanton killing of helpless creatures, I never knew.

If I wasn't playing with friends, I could walk down to Papa's house and see him or one of my uncles. Uncle Frank was my favorite. He taught me how to make a bow and arrows, although I never really got good at using them. When we got a dog, a German Shepherd, Frank named it: Spiegel. Spiegel couldn't have been with us more than a few weeks before he was killed by a truck on the highway.

I remember once watching Frank eat a plate of rice and beans. To this day, I don't think I've ever seen anyone eat with as much obvious enjoyment as Frank ate that meal.

And he taught me words. Frank was the first person I ever heard use the word "tolerate." "I'll not tolerate that behavior," he told me one day, sounding very arch and proper. I don't recall what the behavior was, but I did remember the word, and even had a tolerable understanding of it.

I learned another big word from Frank as well: "telesweer." That's the way it would have been spelled if it had actually been a word, but it wasn't. It was what I heard when Frank would sing the first line of a Nat "King" Cole tune of that time: "They tried to *tell us we're* too young." But I heard "They tried to telesweer too young" and wondered what it meant. I thought it must have been something exciting, because

BEFORE THE BYLINE DON WYCLIFF

adults always seemed to be telling us kids that we were too young to do one thing or another—stay up late, hear a certain song, go to a show—and they were always the things that seemed most exciting.

There was an old man in Dayton, a ragpicker named Mr. Sipp, who pushed a big two-wheeled cart in front of him all around town. If you honked your car horn at him as you passed, he would shout, "Go 'head! You got your gas and lube and your steerin' wheel in your hand!" Every time we would drive past Mr. Sipp, we children would beg Mother or Daddy to punch the car horn. They almost always refused.

I heard someone say many years later that Mr. Sipp had been born a slave and that he had cuts and markings on his ears that indicated who had "owned" him. I'm not sure that was true, since he'd have to have been at least eighty-five years old at that time.

And then there was Parrain. His real name was William "Bud" Bryant, but we called him Parrain—"godfather" in Louisiana Creole French—because he was Grandma's godfather, and that's what she called him. He and his wife, Miss Rosie, lived next door to Grandpa and Grandma at the terminus of a dead-end road on the south end of Dayton. Years later, when I read Alice Walker's novel *The Color Purple*, I thought she surely must have modeled her characters "Mister" and "Celie" after Parrain and Miss Rosie.

Parrain was the brother of "Grandma Lucy," the woman who took in two-year-old Ida Belle Brown and raised her after her own mother, Leana "Lit" Day Brown, died. Parrain had what surely must have been one of the most well-traveled houses in the world. When he found himself squeezed off his own property in the nearby community of Five Mile Settlement, Grandma invited him to move his little three-room house to her property in Dayton. He did, and he and Miss Rosie remained there many years. Then, at some point in the late 1950s, Parrain had a falling-out with Grandma and Grandpa. I'm told it stemmed from Grandpa's rebuking him for the high-handed, threatening way he habitually spoke to Miss Rosie. So he had his house moved back to Five Mile Settlement, to a piece of land owned by a relative of his. After a few years there, he had the house moved back to Dayton, to a spot about half a mile from Grandma's and Grandpa's. After he died in the early 1960s, Grandma invited Miss Rosie to return to her place, which she—and the house—did. The house remained in that spot until Miss Rosie died at age ninety-nine in 1983. It was finally moved to a spot behind Grandma's and Grandpa's house, where it served as a storage shed until it was razed in 2017.

Parrain was already an old man when I first met him. He was of middling height, dark-skinned and, in my recollection, always wore dark pants, a long-sleeved dress shirt and suspenders. Daddy told me he always wore a necktie. He carried a walking stick everywhere he went, but I never knew him to go anywhere but around his own house. That's where we kids would find him when we would go to visit Grandma and Grandpa.

"How's your little health?" he would invariably greet us. He always called Francois "Transfuh" and Karen "Caroline." My name must have been too simple to be mangled or, more likely, played with by this clever old man. He referred to his front porch as "the gallery"—he pronounced it "gal-ry," eliding the middle syllable—and he liked nothing better than to sit there and regale us children with tall tales and pseudo-knowledge.

The land where his and our grandparents' houses sat is at the top of a hill. The hill slopes down for about a hundred yards to a swampy area, wetlands that are part of the Trinity River bottom. The bottom used to be heavily wooded and dense with brush—a genuine thicket. And Parrain delighted in telling us about the "wild man" who lived down in the bottom.

I had no concept then of what a wild man might be or do, but he sounded pretty scary—and that's just what Parrain wanted. I lived for

BEFORE THE BYLINE DON WYCLIFF

years thinking there really was a wild man—a crazy, savage, beast of a man with tattered clothing and untamed hair—living down "under the hill" and waiting to wreak havoc on me and those I loved if we didn't keep a careful eye out for him.

I'm sure Parrain had never been closer to an airplane than the ones we occasionally saw fly over that rural part of Texas—cropdusters, mostly. But he knew exactly how to fly one, and he told us all about it. "If you want to go to St. Louis, you le-e-e-e-an this way," he would say, tilting his upper body to one side. "And if you want to go to New York, you le-e-e-e-an that way," and he would shift in another direction.

Parrain contrived one day to show us how to catch a bird. He took a wooden crate, flipped it bottom up in his bare front yard, and propped one end up with a stick to which he had attached a long string. He sprinkled a little chicken feed on the ground around and under the crate, and then we sat on the gallery, waiting for some hapless sparrow or bluejay or mockingbird to walk under the crate and be trapped when we yanked the stick out. And we waited. And waited. And waited. It had seemed a good idea at the time.

But the person who mattered most to me in Dayton was Grandpa, Socrates "Sprig" Wycliff. I loved the man, and I loved being in his presence. I loved his mannerisms, and I loved the manliness of him. There was nothing he did that didn't intrigue me.

It is hard for me now to separate my perceptions of him before we left Dayton from my perceptions afterwards, the ones I acquired while spending summers with him and Grandma and working with him in his blacksmith shop. But it doesn't really matter much. He was the same Grandpa all the time.

"The shop"—his shop—was a wonderland to me. It must have measured forty feet across the front and about twice that from front to back. It was bisected down the middle by a series of posts, each about ten feet tall. On the post nearest the front hung a green Dr. Pepper clock with the "10", the "2", and the "4" highlighted. Those were the times of day the company advertised as good times to have a Dr. Pepper.

One side of the building—the side west of the posts—was a storage area. The bare ground over there was covered with odd pieces of pipe, angle-iron and other types of metal, and wood in various sizes and shapes. The lighting was dim at best, and, to an outsider, the space looked disorderly. But Grandpa seemed to know, down to the smallest piece, exactly what he had there and precisely where it could be found.

The other side of the shop, the east side, was the main working area. It contained the forge, where Grandpa would heat metal objects—plow points, mower blades, rods, branding irons, all types of implements—and the anvil, where he would hammer the fiery hot metal pieces to sharpen or reshape them. Right next to the front door was an arc welding machine and tanks of acetylene and oxygen, which Grandpa used to join pieces of metal or cut them into pieces, as the task required.

Farther back in the shop were a bandsaw, which always filled me with fear, even when I was much older, and a huge mechanical hammer, which fascinated me. Grandpa used these tools very infrequently. Sometimes when he was away briefly, I would flick the switch and turn the hammer on just to watch the big drive belt go whirring over the wheels that drove the machine. Occasionally, I would even go so far as to put my foot on the lever that engaged the belt and made the hammer go up and down. What power!

Scattered throughout this business side of the shop—hanging from nails hammered into posts, propped against walls or simply "hung up on the ground," as Grandpa liked to joke—were tools of every size, shape and description: wrenches, tongs, chisels, screwdrivers, hammers, measuring devices. Some of them he used every day; some he used almost never. And yet, when he needed a tool, he always seemed to know just where to find it.

At the very back of the shop was a rolltop desk that didn't seem to

BEFORE THE BYLINE DON WYCLIFF

get much use. About the only thing I can remember about it was the pads of invoice sheets imprinted with the words "S. Wycliff and Son."

For a young boy, the shop was a place of mystery, wonder and excitement. I loved going there to watch Grandpa work. Many years later, while on vacation with my wife in the Upper Peninsula of Michigan, we came across a blacksmith shop on Mackinac Island. I walked into the building and was immediately swept away in a tsunami of nostalgia. The smell of coal burning in the forge took me back to the days when I would watch as Grandpa, sweating, bespectacled, and clad in his work "uniform" of blue bib overalls and long-sleeved shirt, would push a piece of cold metal into the coals of his forge and then, a little while later, pull the same piece out, glowing red-hot. Gripping the metal with tongs held in his left hand, he would whirl and position it on the anvil. Then, his lips pursed in concentration, he would begin pounding it with his hammer, a five-pound sledge that he had made for himself. As the metal cooled and reverted to normal color, its shape would be changed under the pressure of Grandpa's hammer blows and taps.

Reflecting on this, I recognized a principle that I have since observed in numerous contexts: It isn't the amount of raw strength one brings to a task that matters; it's the technique one employs in using the strength one has. Grandpa was no muscle man—far from it, he was actually pretty skinny. But he knew how to use the muscle he had and could wield his sledge like an artist wields a brush. He was an artisan who took immense pride in his work. When a new customer would come and ask whether he could fix some broken piece of equipment, he would say, "I'll fix it, or I'll fix it so nobody else can fix it."

Just as interesting as Grandpa's smithing was his talking. Men, both black and white, would come by the shop just for conversation, and the discussions would range from the weather—always a concern in an agricultural area—to the great political issues of the day. I was struck by the fact that Grandpa seemed to speak so freely with the white men who came there. There was no submissive "yes, sir" or "no, sir" as I heard many other black men say routinely when they talked to white men.

I later discerned a lesson in that: Even a black man could enjoy a certain freedom if he had a unique skill or ability that white folks needed. Grandpa was the only blacksmith in that area at that time, and so he was in something of a commanding position. Years later, I would see the same thing demonstrated by Archie Summers, the black cook at the Albert Pick motel restaurant in Terre Haute, Indiana, where I worked as a dishwasher the summer before I started college. "If I don't work, nobody works," Archie used to declare loudly. And he was right.

Grandpa also farmed the twelve acres on which he and Grandma lived south of Dayton, and he raised livestock there as well—cattle, sheep, and chickens. During summertime, he would contract with people who wanted fields mowed to do the mowing in return for the hay. During our teenage years, Francois and I often spent summer days aboard Grandpa's little orange Allis-Chalmers tractor mowing fields and lots for people around Dayton, and then took turns sitting atop a big hay rake to collect the hay into piles. Grandpa, who would have been spending his time at the shop, would come after the raking was done and we would all load the hay onto a trailer, which we would pull behind the tractor to Grandpa's and Grandma's house and deposit in the barn.

When I go to Texas now for summer visits, I wonder how we survived, working as hard as we did in the incinerator that was Texas in summertime. More important, how did Grandpa survive? The man worked harder than anyone I have seen then or since, and he would get up each morning and do it again.

But Grandpa wasn't an all-work-and-no-play kind of guy. He had his enthusiasms and took his pleasures. None of those pleasures was greater than professional wrestling.

BEFORE THE BYLINE DON WYCLIFF

Every Friday night, one of the Houston stations would telecast wrestling matches from the City Auditorium downtown, and Grandpa would always be in his ringside seat: a blue vinyl-covered rocker-recliner in the room where he and Grandma kept the television. Grandma's younger brother, Uncle Clarence Brown, would drive from the north end of town to join Grandpa for the show. And they were a pair to watch!

The names of the wrestlers became familiar to all of us: Gorgeous George; Bull Curry; Danny Savage; Lou Thesz; Dick and Jerry Kozak; Dory Dixon, the rare black wrestler; El Medico, a masked Mexican; Pepper Gomez, small but mighty; Rito Romero, a Mexican lightweight and a favorite of ours; Duke Keomuka, an Asian who was one of the first to learn and apply the excruciatingly painful stomach claw, which meant certain defeat for any opponent who fell victim to it.

I can still hear Grandpa cheering, coaching, exhorting, lamenting, deploring, as he watched the eternal, cosmic conflict between good and evil acted out within the ring at the City Auditorium, while a feckless referee—either Otto Coose or Marvin Jones—struggled to keep a semblance of order and enforce some sort of fairness, and Paul Bosch, the announcer, narrated the proceedings.

"Hit him!" Grandpa would shout when a good guy would win a momentary advantage over his dastardly opponent. "Hit him!"

A few seconds later, of course, the tables would turn as the bad guy pulled some object from his wrestling trunks and used it to blind the hero, or clobber him into senselessness.

"I *told you* to hit him!" Grandpa would wail, the pain in his voice almost palpable, as this disastrous turn of events was acted out.

Somehow, week after week, year after year, the good guys never seemed to figure out that you just couldn't play fair with the baddies, that you had to hit and hit and hit until all the fight was knocked out of them and, maybe most important, that you couldn't expect the referees to do their jobs and enforce fairness and justice.

Besides the wrestling matches, Grandpa watched several other TV shows along with Grandma and Aunt Willie. He especially looked forward to "Lassie." And while I may get my black card pulled for admitting it, we all enjoyed "Amos and Andy."

Grandpa also liked to hunt, and the raccoons that invaded his corn patch annually provided him with a reason to do it. On the best such occasions, he would invite his cousin, Darrell "Son" Trahan, over from Ames to join him. Darrell would show up toward sundown with two or three hounds and a friend or two, and they and Grandpa would disappear into the thicket "under the hill." The dogs would bray; Darrell would urge them on with an exhortation of "Go on aHEAD!" and the hunters would follow them through the soggy bottomland in search of "coons." I was lucky enough to go along with them once or twice. Grandpa carried his shotgun, and I toted a single-shot .22 rifle. I don't recall that we bagged anything on those trips. But for me, the excitement lay in being there, in the presence of these manly men doing a manly thing.

Yes, Grandpa was what I would miss most in leaving Dayton.

But Mother and Daddy had made their decision, and there was no appealing it. We may have been trading "down south," Texas, for "up south," Kentucky, rather than for one of the more glamorous venues that so many other migrating black folks went to, places like New York, Chicago, Seattle, or Los Angeles. But what mattered for us was the same thing that mattered to all the black migrants: The end of our trek promised opportunity, while staying in place meant ... staying in our place, the subordinate station reserved for black folks in the South. And so we went.

BEFORE THE BYLINE DON WYCLIFF

CHAPTER 3
TRANSPLANTING

That first trip to Kentucky was an ordeal on asphalt. We left Dayton on August 26, 1954, a Thursday morning. If my parents' memories were accurate, there were eight of us sardined into our green Chevy Bel Air sedan: three adults—Mother, Grandma, and Grandpa—and five children—Francois, Karen, Chris, Ida, and me. (Daddy was already in Ashland—he had started work there in June; came back briefly in July for the funeral of Papa, mother's father, and then returned to resume his job duties and find a house for us to live in and schools for us children to attend.)

The three adults were crucial because we would be traveling through the South, and this was the era of segregation. Stopping overnight at a motel to rest was not an option, so we needed enough drivers to be able to drive straight through, more than 1,100 miles virtually non-stop.

Additionally, long-distance car travel in those days was immeasurably harder than it is now. There were no divided four-lane interstate highways with convenient rest stops and restaurant facilities. It was all two-lane roads, often with little or no shoulder, so the margin for driver error was narrow to nonexistent. You passed through the middle of every -burg and -ville and metropolis along the way, stopping

BEFORE THE BYLINE DON WYCLIFF

at every red light and hoping not to run afoul of local cops looking to make their ticket quotas by stopping out-of-state drivers going a mile or two over the posted limit. You were at the mercy of every driver of a broken-down jalopy or rickety pickup hauling hay or old furniture or anything else that might come tumbling out of a truckbed. If the driver ahead of you had decided to take a Sunday drive on Thursday, you had to carefully pick your chance to pass him so you could travel at the posted maximum speed.

If you were black, the troubles were compounded. If you needed food, you had to go to the rear of whatever hamburger joint or ice cream stand you stopped at to be served. Most black travelers tried to avoid the need for that by packing plenty of pre-cooked food in their cars, including, almost always, a large supply of fried chicken. The chicken always smelled delicious and mouthwatering at the start of the trip, but by the end, the smell was more likely to induce nausea.

The gas station where you stopped to fill up ("Raglar or ethyl?" the attendant would invariably drawl) might or might not have a restroom for "colored." And especially at night, you had to be on the watch for gangs of "good ole boys" out to have a good time by running black folks off the road—or worse.

We had an added complication on this trip: We were part of a two-vehicle caravan. We were following the truck that carried all our household effects. The truck was owned by a white fellow from Dayton, Herman Payne, who was a friend of Grandma and Grandpa. He had agreed to move our stuff to Ashland for $300. So as we traveled—from Dayton to Beaumont in Texas; through DeQuincy, DeRidder, Leesville, Alexandria, Monroe and Bastrop in Louisiana; up through Greenville in Arkansas; through Clarksdale in the Mississippi delta and on up to Memphis, Humboldt and Clarksville in Tennessee, and finally into Kentucky, through Bowling Green to Elizabethtown to Bardstown and Versailles to Lexington, Winchester, Morehead, Grayson and, lastly and mercifully, Ashland—we were constantly trying to keep up with Herman's truck. It was driven alternately by him, his wife Muriel, and Uncle Sam Wickliff, Grandpa's youngest brother, who was an auto mechanic and was recruited as a third driver for the truck.

As the adults took turns driving, we children took turns being carsick and, especially after we got into the rolling hills and mountains of eastern Kentucky, throwing up. (In later years on other trips we learned how to deal with that problem: We ate saltine crackers all the time. As long as you were forcing something down your gullet, nothing could come up.) And when we got antsy, the adults would distract us with a game: See if you can spot the billowing tarp over the bed of Herman's truck ahead of us.

We got to Ashland early on Saturday, August 28, and found our way to the house at the south end of town that Daddy had rented for us. I don't remember much about the house except that it was on a hill and the front yard sloped steeply down to a sidewalk and the street. I recall being amazed that we were going to be living on a paved street with sidewalks next to it, instead of a highway with drainage ditches on the sides, or on a dirt road.

Daddy and the three other men promptly began unloading the truck and placing things in the house. Mother recalled that they were almost finished when, abruptly, everything came to a stop. A strange white man showed up at the front door and began talking with Daddy. Mother said she couldn't hear what was being said at first, but saw that Daddy began to look "downhearted."

She walked to the front door where Daddy and the man were standing.

"What's the matter?" she asked.

Daddy explained that the man was the landlord, and he was saying that some of the neighbors had called him and complained when they saw a "colored" family moving in. As far as he was concerned, the landlord said, we could stay in the house, but he couldn't know what the neighbors might do.

That was no consolation to Daddy, who replied, "How do you think I would feel going off to work every day knowing my family may be in danger?"

Under these circumstances, Mother and Daddy both realized we couldn't remain in the house; they would have to find another. But we would have to stay in this house at least until they could find a new one. The landlord suggested that Daddy go to the police and ask them to keep a special eye on the place as long as we were there.

At this point, Herman spoke up. It is important to appreciate who Herman Payne was. If you had been a Hollywood casting director looking for someone to play the quintessential redneck, you couldn't have picked anyone better than Herman. Big, redheaded, not particularly well-educated, he was a workingman, scuffling to make a living however he could. He and Muriel had a passel of children, and I still remember going to their house for a visit one night before we moved away from Dayton. They had an old piano and someone played it while everybody sang, "Hail, Hail, the Gang's All Here." (I remember it so well because, once again, a word tripped me up. I thought everybody was singing "Hell, Hell, the Gang's All Here," and it gave me a thrill to hear everybody singing so lustily this word we children were forbidden to speak.)

Anyway, pointing to Mother, who was five months pregnant with the baby who would be my sister Joy, Herman addressed the landlord. "This woman has been on the road for three days," he said, "and she's in no condition to be moving anywhere tonight. Now I'm gonna spend the night in my truck out back with my shotgun, and if anybody comes around here trying to mess with these people, they're gonna have to deal with me."

And he did.

Daddy went to the police and told them about the situation. The police said there had been no racial incidents in that part of town, but they agreed to keep a special watch on the house that night.

The next day, Sunday, Daddy and the other men went out to look for another house. Daddy had previously noticed a vacant house on Central Avenue, also in south Ashland, but had been unable to find anyone who could show him the place or tell him how much the rent might be. On this Sunday, however, luck was with him. He knocked on the door of the house next door and found the residents home. It turned out that the lady of the house, Christine Kinney, was handling the showing and renting of the place for the owner, who lived in Cincinnati.

Mrs. Kinney—"Miss Chris" we children later learned to call her—showed him the place. Daddy rented it on the spot, and we moved in that same day. There was no need to spend another night at the house on the hill, no need for Herman Payne to sleep in his truck, cradling his shotgun.

That house, at 3137 Central Avenue, was our home for the next four years. Like every other house we lived in, it was too small—living room, kitchen, two bedrooms, one bath. But that was par for the course in those days of big families and little affluence. Our parents had one bedroom, the girls had another, where Chris also slept. Francois and I shared a foldout couch in the living room.

The living room had a mantle, something I had never seen before, and a fireplace that we never used. There was a porch that wrapped around both the front and the south side of the house. The yard—a big one with a tall apple tree in the center—was on the north side.

Most important, the house was safe. The neighbors to the south and east were black, those to the north and west were white. There was no friction in the neighborhood. There would be no racial danger here. Safely housed at last, we children still needed to be schooled. And so on Monday morning, not yet twenty-four hours in the new house, Mother took Francois, Karen and me to enroll us for the first time in Catholic school. It would also be the first time that Francois and I would attend school with white children.

I had finished first grade and Francois had finished fifth in June at Colbert Elementary School in Dayton. In Ashland, as in Dayton, the public schools were segregated. Had we gone to public school, we would have enrolled at Booker T. Washington, the colored school in Ashland. This, even though the U.S. Supreme Court had ruled four months earlier, on May 17, 1954, that separate but equal had no place in public education in the U.S. It would be half a dozen years before public schools in Ashland were integrated. But Daddy, impatient with Jim Crow and all his inequities and indignities, didn't want to wait.

It was his boss at the prison, Walter Graybeal, who suggested that he look into sending us to Catholic school. "You're Catholic, aren't you, Wyc?" he asked. "Well, why don't you send your kids to Catholic school just like anybody else would?"

Daddy knew it wasn't as simple as doing "just like anybody else would." But he liked the idea and decided to go and see if his black Catholic children really could attend Holy Family School. It was early August when he went and knocked on the door of the parish rectory on Winchester Avenue in north Ashland. The housekeeper answered the door, and Daddy asked to speak to the pastor. Within a few minutes, he was talking with Monsignor Declan Carroll.

With his florid face, snow white hair and unmistakably Irish brogue, Father Carroll was another of those characters who could have been sent from central casting. He was, in fact, an Irish immigrant, born in 1886 in the village of Clashmore in County Waterford on the southern coast of Ireland. He and his family moved to the United States around 1897. They settled in Covington in northern Kentucky, just across the Ohio River from Cincinnati. Young Declan attended St. Xavier High School and then St. Xavier College in Cincinnati. He went on to St.

Thomas College at the Catholic University of America from 1906 to 1910. In 1911, he attended St. Mary Seminary in Baltimore as a student for the Diocese of Covington. He was ordained on June 21, 1911, by Cardinal James Gibbons of Baltimore and returned to Covington.

Daddy told him that he was new to Ashland, that he was employed at the Federal Correctional Institution, that he was Catholic and that he wanted to enroll his children in the parish school. Without hesitation, Monsignor Carroll replied, "I don't see why your children can't attend our school." But just to be sure, he said, let him confer with the bishop in Covington. He promised to call Daddy at work the following Wednesday.

On Tuesday, Daddy said, he was summoned to his departmental office to take a phone call. It was Father Carroll.

"Mr. Wycliff, the bishop says that the Catholic schools are for all Catholic children," the priest said. "Your children will be welcome in our school."

At that point, the old priest could have congratulated himself and gone back to business as usual. But he didn't. A few weeks later—on that very Sunday when Daddy was scrambling to find us a new place to live— Monsignor Carroll took to the pulpit at Mass and made an announcement. According to one of Daddy's colleagues at the prison, Carroll told his parishioners that there were going to be "colored children" attending the parish school that fall and that he wanted them treated with decency and respect. And if anyone did not do so, he said, that person would be denied the sacraments of the church.

Many years later, when I was a member of The New York Times editorial board, I would write a commentary in which I cited Father Carroll's behavior in this situation as an example of courageous leadership by a churchman.

Mother was aware of none of that, however, as she stood with Francois, Karen and me at the school that Monday morning. What she was aware of, she said, were news reports about black children in another Kentucky town, Sturgis, being "stoned" as they tried to integrate their local public school. "I thought," she said, "that they might try to stone me."

The registration site was the convent, where the Sisters of Divine Providence, who staffed Holy Family School, lived. The convent had a large, screened front porch where mothers and their children congregated to wait to register. Mother nervously approached the building, opened the door and took a position near it, with her back against a wall and her three children drawn in close—in case, she said, she needed to make a quick escape.

For several minutes, no one said anything, either hostile or welcoming. And then, a lady standing with a little girl on the opposite side of the porch approached.

The woman smiled and asked, "What is your little girl's name?"

"Karen," Mother replied nervously. "Karen Wycliff."

"Why, that's my daughter's name, too!" the lady exclaimed. Then, turning to her daughter, she said, "Karen Horgan, meet Karen Wycliff."

The woman's name was Virginia Horgan, and her gesture of friendship broke the ice for Mother and dispelled her fears of being stoned or spurned. "You'll never know what a smile can mean to a person," Mother used to say when she recalled that day.

Her anxiety was relieved, but she wasn't the only one with concerns. I was full of anxiety, and I'm sure Francois must have been also. My fears came to the fore on the first day of classes, when Sister Helen Joseph marched our second-grade class over to the church for Mass. Half the class filed into pews on one side of the center aisle, and the other half went to the other side. Whether because my last name began with a "W" or because I was tall or for some other reason entirely, I was at the back of the formation on the left side.

After Mass, we were supposed to file out of our seats into the middle aisle, genuflect, and then walk out with a partner who would be coming from a pew on the opposite side of the aisle. As the children in the rows ahead of me filed out, my anxiety grew. Would I have a partner, or would I be all alone? What if none of these new people, these *white* people, wanted to walk with me?

Suddenly, it was my row that was moving out into the aisle. And then it was my turn. I stepped out of my pew, genuflected and looked to my right, where my partner should be. And there was a boy, about my height, with dark, crew-cut hair, waiting to walk out with me. His name was Johnny Thompson, and it turned out that he and his big family lived just a few doors north of us on Central Avenue. He liked to play army, and he liked "Ike," President Dwight Eisenhower. I didn't care about Ike, but I liked Johnny, that day and always, because he was my partner and I was not left to walk alone.

Even after that episode, my anxieties about my new circumstances were not over. After the first marking period, I brought home a report card on which Sister Helen Joseph noted that I didn't participate much in class discussions, didn't associate with my classmates and was, in general, not fitting in.

Daddy took me aside one night for a conversation about this. I recall sitting with him at the table in our green-walled kitchen as he asked me gently what was wrong. I don't recall that I had a coherent answer for him. I think he already knew that I was full of fear of my new surroundings—the city, the school, the people, the novel experience of being so much among white people—and full of longing for my old surroundings: my cousin Sam Brown and my friends, Grandma and Grandpa and their house and farm, Dayton and all it represented in terms of home.

What has stuck with me through all my years was one question that Daddy asked: Would you like to go back to Dayton and live with Grandma and Grandpa and go to school there?

The answer to that one was easy. Yes—and no. Of course, I would like to go back, but I didn't want to be separated from him and Mother and all of my brothers and sisters. Seven years old is too young to struggle with such a dilemma.

Of course, I don't think Daddy would have sent me back to Dayton anyway. I know that now. But I didn't know it then.

Somehow, after that conversation, I began to find my footing at Holy Family and in Ashland. Over time, I made friends in class and became a good student. But God! How hard those early days were!

They must have been even harder for Francois, who was just at the threshold of adolescence when we moved and who had been accustomed to spending as much time at Grandma's and Grandpa's house as at ours in Dayton. I once tried to ask Francois about that move and his feelings about it, and his response left no doubt in my mind that he felt cheated by having been forced to move. He wouldn't talk about it much.

Of the three of us who were in school that year, Karen, I think, had the easiest time. She had not been in school previously and so had no old patterns and expectations to overcome. She quickly made friends in addition to Karen Horgan. She became the mascot for the seventh and eighth-grade cheerleading squad. And she thrived.

Ultimately, all of us thrived academically. We learned to "talk proper"—pronouncing "er" in the standard American way instead of as "uh," the Brooklyn, Boston and African American way. In Dayton, I had been one of the better students in my first-grade class, but Sister Helen Joseph made me a bluebird instead of a cardinal in her reading groups. I distinctly recall being upset about this and put a whip to my horses to get into the top group, the cardinals.

With Mother's enthusiastic approval, Sister Helen Joseph also converted me from writing with my left hand to writing with my right. Among her other beliefs, Mother was convinced that one was in some way deficient if one was left-handed. So she had the good sister perform a conversion. I have always felt as if that forced change left me in some measure permanently confused.

Francois, who had taken piano lessons for several years already, thrived as a piano student under Sister Mary Herman, the music teacher at Holy Family.

Mother used to relate how some of the other mothers in the school asked her one day whether she allowed us to watch television. Yes, she replied. The other women said they thought that perhaps she did not, because it was well-known that the Wycliff children were among the smartest in their classes, and they thought it probably was because we didn't watch TV.

In fact, we were avid TV watchers. But we were equally avid readers, thanks to the Sisters of Divine Providence. Those nuns were motivational geniuses, using fancily decorated "holy cards" and slogans like "Readers are Leaders" to inculcate in us and our classmates a love of reading. I remember my fourth-grade teacher, Sister John Catherine, reading aloud to us in class in brief installments a book called "Outlaws of Ravenhurst." I could hardly wait for each new day to hear what came next in that book.

The reading habit planted in us by the nuns was fertilized by the presence in Ashland of a public library where there was no color bar, unusual for the time. Karen and I first, and later Chris, fell in love with a series of biographies of famous (and some not-so-famous) Americans. Each book had a blue cover and was emblazoned with the name of the subject—*Zebulon Pike: Explorer, George Washington Carver: Scientist*, and so forth. For months, we went to the library in Central Park and brought home one, two, three of these biographies at a time. At some point, Daddy (Karen says it was Mother, but I recall it was Daddy) grew tired of seeing those blue-backed books and felt we needed to vary our reading. So he declared that he didn't want to see another of those blue books come into the house. "Read something else!" he ordered.

We quickly discovered that the library carried the same series with orange covers, and shifted to those. Our hunger for biographies was satisfied, and Daddy's desire for variety in our reading was frustrated—by a simple change of colors.

There was one gap in our Holy Family experience—at least in mine and Francois'—and that was in relationships with members of the opposite sex. The proscription against interracial romantic relationships, or even just boy-girl friendships, was something neither Father Carroll nor anyone else could—or would—knock down in that era. And if that wasn't clear to us before, it was unmistakably clear after the lynching of Emmett Till in 1955.

What happened to "that Till boy" became one of those chilling object lessons that black adults recited and black youth absorbed about the racial shape of the world. As a result, I think, Francois and I both grew up stunted to some degree. I know that he was attracted to certain young women in his class, but dating or even being friends with them was out of the question. It was the same for me. When all the boys in my class fell in love with the "It Girl" of a particular moment, I kept my silence and my distance. That was life.

CHAPTER 4
ASHLAND DAYS

We called her Apple Girl. She must have had a real name, of course, but Apple Girl is the only name by which we ever knew her. She was skinny, had dishwater blonde hair, and was a year or two older than I. In the fall, when the apples on the big tree in our yard would ripen, she would appear every few days at our back door carrying a battered white dishpan.

"Could we have some of those apples?" she would inquire of whichever Wycliff opened the door in response to her knock. Her wording never varied.

At first, we kids would go and dutifully ask Mother. But after a time, we knew what Mother's answer would be, so we just said yes. The tree bore far more apples than even our big family could use. And besides, Mother would always say, "They're probably worse off than we are."

I don't know how "bad off" Apple Girl's family was. I don't even know how many of them there were. They lived a few doors north of us and across the alley, facing Railroad Street. We never played with them as we occasionally did with Mitchell and Sandy Stapleton, the white kids who lived in the house just north of ours on our street, Central Avenue.

BEFORE THE BYLINE DON WYCLIFF

I also didn't know how "bad off" we were. I certainly knew we were not rich. Many were the mornings when we scoured the house for a nickel or a penny for bus fare or to be able to buy lunch at school. But we never wanted for food, and I just assumed that everybody in our circle of friends and acquaintances—everybody black, anyway—lived about as we did.

That meant we each had a set of Sunday clothes—clean, creased trousers, sport coat, white shirt, tie and dress shoes for each of the boys, even the youngest; a nice dress, patent leather shoes and a hat for each of the girls—plus a modest number of other clothes to knock about in. In Texas, that had meant bib overalls, blue jeans, or, as one photograph of me shows, shorts with suspenders, along with a pair of high-top tennis shoes. In Kentucky, the bib overalls disappeared, but the rest remained. Because we went to Catholic schools, we didn't have to worry about what to wear there: Everybody wore uniforms—navy blue skirts and white blouses for the girls; dark trousers and white shirts for the boys. And no tennis shoes.

Our diet was pretty basic. Lots of ground beef and chicken. Mother and Daddy used to laugh about how they would buy chicken backs on sale at the A&P and then ask each of us at dinner which piece of the chicken we'd like. The joke was that no matter what you answered, you ended up with a chicken back. And with the possible exception of Francois, we were all too young to catch on. Ignorance truly can be bliss.

I do recall that after we moved to Kentucky, our diets changed somewhat. I had grown up thinking that syrup was Uncle Timme's incomparable cane syrup, which came in silver-colored gallon cans and which we would decant into smaller serving vessels. In Ashland, syrup became Karo corn syrup. Ugh! What a disappointment! In Texas, we had rice at virtually every meal. In Kentucky, it seemed Mother began serving potatoes and pasta (usually macaroni and cheese) more often.

But the biggest changes, for me, were in what we didn't have. In

Texas, Mother would occasionally fry sweet potato slices—Grandpa grew sweet potatoes—and would make lemon meringue and chocolate pies. Those delights grew scarce after we moved to Kentucky. That probably had less to do with money than with time and Mother's workload. Joy, the sixth child in the family, was born on January 5, 1955, about four months after we arrived in Ashland. Mother had her hands more than full.

Daddy told me that when we moved from Dayton to Ashland, his salary nearly doubled, from just under $2,200 a year as a teacher in Orange to $3,975 as an instructor in the prison at Ashland. Even given the difference in the cost of living, that represented a considerable step up in income—a step onto a low rung of the middle class.

But I recall feeling deeply uneasy in Ashland, as if our financial life as a family was always precarious. In Dayton, it seemed, we had been surrounded by people on whom we could rely for help—black people and white. I recall one day going with Mother to Remke's grocery store in Dayton. We got to the checkout, and she found she didn't have enough cash. "Charge it," she said to the clerk, and we walked out with the few items she had purchased. In Ashland, I sensed, there was nobody who knew us, nobody to whom one could say, "Charge it."

We had been a pretty devout Catholic family before we moved, but once in Ashland and at Holy Family, our devotional life was ratcheted up several notches. One night Mother heard the rosary being recited on a local radio station, so we began praying the rosary every night as a family. Sometime after dinner, usually when a really good TV program was just starting, Mother would issue her call to prayer: "The Holy Rosary!" We would all gather in the living room and assume the position: on our knees in front of a shrine stationed on the living room mantel. The centerpiece of the shrine was a reproduction of Michelangelo's "Pieta," with the Blessed Virgin cradling the broken body of the dead Jesus across her lap. Needless to say, both the Virgin and Jesus were white.

BEFORE THE BYLINE DON WYCLIFF

Religious devotion even became part of our play as children. Occasionally, we would play "Mass," with Francois or me as the celebrant (hey, it had to be a guy) and the rest of the kids reciting the Latin liturgy. Mother had a green cape that she used to put around our necks to catch hair when she gave us haircuts. Our celebrant would don the cape, letting it hang down his back instead of the front. Because we both were altar servers, Francois and I got used to the mannerisms of each of the parish priests as they would say Mass, and we imitated our favorites. I particularly liked the way Father Haney used to whirl around to face the congregation when the old liturgy called for it, and I used to try to make my green "chasuble" billow in just the way his real one did.

Our family entertainment consisted most memorably of Sunday drives. In those days of cheap gasoline, we would all pile into the Chevy and Daddy would drive. Sometimes we would cross the bridge over the Ohio River and go westward alongside it, to a spot not far from Ironton, where there was a shrine to Our Lady of Fatima. Sometimes we would go as far east as Gallipolis, Ohio, and watch the water spill endlessly over the dam there. Other times, we would drive to the airport in Huntington, West Virginia, to watch planes—Piedmont and Allegheny were the two airlines that served Huntington at that time—take off and land.

Occasionally, we would go to Dawson Park, a gathering place for blacks in Ashland. There was a swimming pool at the park, and my one experience of it provided me with my lifelong fear of deep water. The first time we went there, I raced out of the dressing room and leapt into the center of the pool. Instantly, I was in over my head, suspended between the floor of the pool and the surface of the water, and unable to propel myself. I kept trying to breathe, but all I could manage to inhale was water. I was drowning. I finally managed to grab the leg of someone sitting at the edge of the pool and pull myself over. Suddenly, Daddy was leaning over the side, pulling me out, laying me across his knee, raising and lowering my arms to clear my lungs of water and fill them with air. I have been terrified of deep water ever since that day, and have never learned to swim.

Very occasionally, our family would go to the movies at the Trail Drive-in Theatre on U.S. Highway 60 just outside of Ashland. The downtown indoor theatres—the Capitol and the Paramount—were off limits to blacks except one day a year. But the drive-in was always available, and the whole family could get in for one price. Almost always, we saw movies with religious themes, like *The Song of Bernadette, A Man Called Peter* or *The Robe*. The one non-religious film I can remember seeing was *Imitation of Life*. I'm not sure I understood what it was about, but it had a black character in a key role, and that made it important.

But for the most part, we stayed around home. Like a growing number of Americans at that time, we had acquired a television set— our first one was a castoff black-and-white unit from Grandma and Grandpa—and had become avid watchers. Truth is, our appetite for TV far exceeded the available supply of programming, since the only dependably viewable station at that time in Ashland was WSAZ, Channel 3 ("with studios in Huntington and Charleston, West Virginia," the announcer would intone). Unfortunately, WSAZ didn't carry the show that we kids most desired to see, *The Mickey Mouse Club*. We were forced to watch a grainy transmission of it on another channel, whose call letters I can't remember. On WSAZ we watched the local after-school show for kids, hosted by a character called "Aunt Drusilla" (inevitably, we pronounced it Dru-silly). On weekends there was the country music show *Saturday Night Jamboree* ("... brought to you by the Ashland Oil & Refining Co. ... And here he is, your old country cousin, Dean Sturm!") and the national broadcast of *Your Hit Parade*, sponsored by Lucky Strike cigarettes ("L.S.M.F.T.—Lucky Strike Means Fine Tobacco"). We kids liked to stage our own performances of

BEFORE THE BYLINE DON WYCLIFF

the show at home.

Saturday morning was a feast for kids with, among other programs, *Andy's Gang*, which included a serial featuring two turbaned Indian characters named Gunga and Rama; *Fury* ("the story of a horse, and the boy who loved him"); *Howdy Doody*, (my first crush was on Princess Summerfallwinterspring), and *Circus Boy*, whose title character was played by Mickey Dolenz, who turned up in the 1960s as a member of the singing group The Monkees.

For kids, Sunday was a TV desert. There was *The Gospel Harmony Boys* ("Someone to care, someone to share, all your troubles, like no other can do") and a program whose purpose I simply couldn't understand, *Meet the Press*. I don't recall where in the TV lineup *Flatt and Scruggs* came, but we watched it often enough that bluegrass became one of my favorite kinds of music. I can still today sing the commercial jingle for Martha White flour (with "Hot Rize").

But my favorite TV viewing was Major League Baseball. The games were broadcast on Saturday afternoons and announced by the former Brooklyn Dodgers' great Pee Wee Reese and the old St. Louis Cardinals' pitcher Dizzy Dean. I loved listening to "Old Diz," with his fractured syntax and his malapropisms—"he slud into third base"—and his exuberance—"He was goin' for the downs on that one, Pee Wee. He really had a ripple!"

And when I wasn't watching baseball, I usually was playing it, more often than not with Wilson Barrow, whose large family lived directly behind ours in a house that faced Railroad Street. Wilson, who was at least two years older than I, was a talented natural athlete and an attractive nuisance to me. I recognized his talent, and so I wanted to compete with him—at baseball, marbles, whatever. But I hated that he *always* beat me, no matter what game we played. I would no sooner get a few new marbles than Wilson would relieve me of them, adding them to the hundreds he already had in a big glass jug that he used to hoist onto his right shoulder. The thought of saving myself anguish by *not* playing with Wilson never occurred to me. I wanted to be able to throw a baseball as hard and accurately as he could. I wanted to shoot marbles as well as he did. But I never could, and the frustration of always losing to him often brought me to tears. And that's when Wilson would pile on with a derisive taunt, "Baaaby. Big baby!" Oh, how it hurt!

Our neighborhood was an odd one. On our block of Central Avenue, all the houses north of us were occupied by white people, including my classmate John Thompson and his big family. All the houses south of us, with one notable exception, were occupied by black people: "Mr. Bill" and "Miss Chris" Kinney next door (Mr. Bill, who had been injured in the Navy in World War II, always drove a late-model Buick with curb feelers, so he could avoid scraping his whitewall tires against the curb); the Barrows (they were related somehow to Wilson's family, and their teenage daughter Sharon was, I believed, the second-most beautiful girl in the world at that time); the Washingtons (their daughter Jackie was the most beautiful girl in the world) and so on down to the Honakers, Chester and Pauline, who had no children at the time but later adopted a son, David. The last house at the south end of the block was occupied by an elderly white man, Carl P. Tackett, and his wife. Mr. Tackett ran a small grocery store out of his house, selling bread, milk and assorted other basic items, including candies. We children were avid customers at Tackett's Grocery—as avid as our extremely limited funds would allow.

If memory serves me correctly, Railroad Street behind us followed the same racial pattern. Everything north of the Barrows' house was white; everything south of it was black. Apple Girl's family lived on Railroad Street—so named because the Chesapeake & Ohio railroad tracks ran directly parallel to the street right through the neighborhood. Karen and I—"Motorcycle Girl" and "Motorcycle Boy," we styled ourselves—liked to ride Francois' bike up and down Railroad

BEFORE THE BYLINE DON WYCLIFF

Street. I would pedal the bike, and Karen would ride on the handlebars, and neither of us wore a helmet or any kind of protective gear. I recall we took more than one spill, and I wonder now how we managed to get through those years without at least one skull fracture between us.

One event stands out above all others from those Central Avenue days. It happened on a Saturday. Mother and Daddy took me with them to go shopping in downtown Ashland. Francois was left in charge of the other kids at home. Our last stop on that trip was at Ashland Dry Goods, a department store downtown. Mother and Daddy went inside and left me outside in the car. That wasn't unusual in those days.

When they finally emerged and got into the car, they were smiling broadly, and Mother was carrying a brown paper bag. Something was up, but I didn't know what. Mother began singing "Take Me Out to the Ballgame," and both she and Daddy looked back at me from the front seat. Finally, I could take it no more. I grabbed the bag that Mother had placed on the floor of the back seat and opened it. Inside were two baseball mitts, one of pretty good quality and the other a flat, pancakey kind of thing. One, I realized, would be mine, and one would be for Chris. I picked the good one and immediately began pounding a pocket into it. At that moment, I think, I was about as happy as a kid could possibly be. It wasn't until I became a parent myself that I appreciated what Mother and Daddy must have been feeling at that moment. It can't be described; it can only be felt.

I felt such happiness one other time during our Ashland years. It was the summer of 1958, the year after the Milwaukee Braves had defeated the New York Yankees in the World Series. Daddy drove the whole family to Cincinnati, 125 miles up the Ohio River, to attend a Major League Baseball game in person at Crosley Field, then the home of the Cincinnati Redlegs. I have never forgotten that day. I don't think Francois wanted to be there—he didn't care much for baseball, or any sport for that matter. I don't know what the other kids were thinking.

Mother was worried about the expense of the trip. But I was in heaven.

It was a gorgeous, sunny day. We sat high up in the left field stands—about as far from home plate as one could have gotten. But as far as I was concerned, we were in the thick of the action. I couldn't believe that I was in the same stadium, breathing the same air, as the baseball heroes I had seen only on TV to that point in my life—the great Hank Aaron and Wes Covington for the Braves, Frank Robinson and Vada Pinson for the Redlegs. Life was excellent.

* * *

It was about that same time, in 1958, that we moved from the house on Central Avenue to a new house at 2017 Hilton Avenue, farther north and closer to downtown. I didn't realize it at the time, but Mother and Daddy had bought the new house, which stood across the street from a steep hill covered with trees, rocks and brush. We kids and our friends spent many happy hours climbing and exploring on that hill, and hiding out beneath "Big Rock," a massive stone outcropping created eons earlier while the Appalachian Mountain range was in formation.

Our next-door neighbors on Hilton were, on one side, a fellow named Tom Jordan and, on the other, an elderly couple named Anderson. Mr. Jordan, who was probably in his mid-fifties, was a sour character, perpetually grumpy and not fond of children. I seem to recall that he was a widower, and he seemed not to have many friends. Not only did he seem unhappy with his life, but he seemed determined to squelch others' happiness. I recall a day when a friend and I were tossing a rubber ball on the sidewalk in front of our house, and the ball hit his car. He called the police. They came and calmed him down, but not before I had been thoroughly traumatized by the thought of being hauled off to jail. Already then, I knew that the police were no laughing matter.

BEFORE THE BYLINE DON WYCLIFF

Mr. and Mrs. Anderson were an interesting pair. They both were old, probably in their late sixties. Mr. Anderson was tall and light-skinned and was always dressed in a suit and tie. He suffered from what I now know must have been dementia or Alzheimer's disease. Everybody in the neighborhood knew that he could not be allowed to leave his yard. One of our humorous family stories is about a day when Mr. Anderson made a break for it. He was walking down the sidewalk in front of our house when my sister Ida, a skinny little girl of no more than six or seven, spotted him. She ran out to the sidewalk to head him off. Waving her arms and steadily retreating as the old man advanced, Ida shouted repeatedly, "Go back, Mr. Anderson! Go back!"

She couldn't turn him around, but her shouts alerted the grownups, who came and took Mr. Anderson in hand and led him back home.

Mrs. Anderson was short, very dark-skinned, and very angry. What I remember most about her was her dog, Ponto. The dog looked to be a cocker spaniel or something similar, and his disposition was like that of his mistress—angry and mean. Grownups in the neighborhood used to say that Mrs. Anderson fed the dog raw meat to make it vicious. I don't know whether either part of that proposition is true—that she fed the dog raw meat or that eating raw meat makes a dog vicious. I just know that I tried to steer clear of Mrs. Anderson *and* Ponto.

Just beyond the Andersons' house was that of the Foleys—L.J. and Josephine and their five children: Johnny, Jerry, Jimmy, Dawn, and Denise. Johnny was a year or two older than I, Jerry was a year or two younger, and Jimmy was about a year younger than Jerry. Dawn and Denise were roughly the same ages as my sisters, Ida and Joy.

Johnny and Jerry instantly became my best playmates. Neither of them was the athlete that Wilson Barrow was, so baseball, which we played perpetually in the alley behind our houses, was more enjoyable and less stressful to me. Jerry had a stupendously foul mouth for a boy of his age. Jimmy was kind of a cypher to me. Dawn was dark-haired.

Denise probably was prettier, but both were too young for me to care about. Johnny had a bad stutter and the hots for Karen, who refused to have anything to do with him.

Somewhere farther up the street from the Foleys lived a white kid named Lon Castle. I knew little about him except that he seemed rich—he always had the latest toys, including things like a motorized go-kart—and he seemed not to have any friends. He would come down the alley to where the Foley kids and Chris and I played our endless baseball games, and he seemed to want our friendship. But he seemed to want us to join him in playing with his toys, while we wanted only to play baseball. So no spark of friendship ever got struck.

BEFORE THE BYLINE DON WYCLIFF

CHAPTER 5
RACE

One day, when I was in about the fourth grade, Mother picked me up after school instead of having me ride the bus home. There was a boy in my class—I don't remember his first name, but his last name was Dickman—who also lived toward the south end of Ashland and needed a ride home. Mother agreed to give him one, so he piled into the back seat of the car along with me.

As we approached Dickman's neighborhood, he turned to me and asked, "What's your mom's first name?" I had no idea why he wanted to know, and it never occurred to me to ask.

"Emily," I told him.

He promptly turned toward the front seat and said, "Emily, you can let me off at the next corner."

I don't remember Mother's response, but I immediately picked up the tautness in her voice that signaled she was angry and I was in trouble.

As soon as Dickman got out of the car and slammed the door shut, Mother lit into me. "How did that boy know my first name?" she asked.

"He asked me and I told him," I replied, hoping the simple, unvarnished truth would save me.

"Well, you listen to me, boy!" she hissed. "The next time somebody

BEFORE THE BYLINE DON WYCLIFF

asks you my name, you tell them it's *Mrs.* Wycliff! They can put a handle in front of my name just like they do for a white woman!"

I knew better than to try to explain further. Dickman, the little dweeb, had touched one of the deepest sensitivities a black person possesses: the abhorrence of being disrespected by a white person. It would have been bad enough if a white grownup had spoken to Mother that way, but a child? Intolerable! And since I had foolishly enabled him, I took the brunt of her anger for both of us.

Even at that young age, I understood the reason for Mother's anger. But I didn't appreciate the reason for her ferocity until many years later, when we were talking one day about her upbringing in segregated Texas.

"We were brought up having to call white girls our age 'Miss,'" she told me. "*We really thought they were better than we were.*"

Those may have been the saddest words I ever heard Mother speak.

Daddy described something similar as he related an incident from his childhood. It was a hot summer day when he was in second or third grade, and he asked his father for a nickel to buy an ice cream cone.

"I went to the drug store to buy the ice cream," he said. "After ordering, I climbed up on a stool at the counter, and Mr. McGinty [the store owner] promptly told me to get down, that colored people could not sit in his store. I got my ice cream and went skipping away just as happy as if nothing had happened. *I didn't think about being offended; that was the way of life.*"

For a black person in America, race is like your shadow: You can never outrun it, escape it, divest yourself of it. It is always there—sometimes a large presence, sometimes a smaller one; sometimes dark and foreboding, sometimes not; sometimes racism, sometimes just ... race.

Nothing is more absurd and angering to me than to hear white commentators lecture black people about putting race behind them, letting bygones be bygones. As if centuries of slavery and segregation and all that went with them were just some dispute among neighbors about a fence line or a limb hanging over your driveway. Hey, just let it go! It's in the past.

And yes, in a way it is. But it never will be fully behind us, any more than our shadows will be. In America, you can't outrun race.

For black people, the stories we tell ourselves and our children about race and racism are part of our cultural capital: resources necessary for survival in the world. One would no more allow one's child to leave home and venture into the world without such capital than one would send him or her out on a subfreezing day without a proper coat. Those stories are useful history; they can help our young avoid trouble or cope with it when it inevitably comes; they can also propel them to greater achievement.

And so here is some of my cultural capital.

The first time I can recall anyone calling me "nigger" was in first grade. It was a classmate in my segregated colored school in Dayton who did it.

I went to our teacher, a woman who was a close friend and colleague of my grandmother and a highly respected figure in the black community of Dayton, and told her what my classmate had called me. "Well," she replied, "that's what you are, aren't you?"

Even though I was young, I already understood that she wasn't really asking me a question. Some years later, I realized she was also telling me something else entirely: Don't be a tattletale. But that realization came only after I had puzzled for a long time over the oddness of having my black teacher affirm that, "Yes, Don Wycliff, you are a nigger."

The most painful racial incident of my childhood happened not to me directly, but to one of the people I loved most, my mother, because of me. I was in sixth or maybe seventh grade and had been chosen as captain of the school safety patrol at Holy Family. We were the kids who strapped on white shoulder belts and stood on the corners near the school, helping children cross the streets safely before and after classes. Since Holy Family enrolled both elementary and high school children, we probably weren't really needed, but we took our duties seriously.

It was customary at the end of the school year for all the safety patrol members from all the schools in the area to be treated to a day of fun at Camden Park, the amusement park in nearby Huntington, West Virginia. There was just one problem: Camden Park did not routinely admit black people.

I say routinely because the prohibition against blacks was not inflexible. When the annual Holy Family parish outing was held at Camden Park, our family was admitted right along with all the other members of the parish. And once a year, the Armco Steel Co. employees had an outing at Camden Park, and black employees and their families were admitted.

But Father Carroll, our champion at Holy Family, had died in 1957 and been replaced by a new pastor, and there was a new principal of the school as well, and these newcomers perhaps had not yet learned to call the segregationists' bluff. In any case, the new principal got word that I could not be admitted to Camden Park with the rest of the safety patrollers, and she had to call my parents to let them know.

I was at home, sitting in the kitchen having an after-school snack, when the call came. Our phone hung on a kitchen wall, and I watched and listened as Mother, standing with her back to the wall, answered it. It was largely a one-way conversation, the nun doing most of the talking and Mother replying, periodically, "Yes, Sister." As the conversation went on, Mother began to cry, and then to slump toward the floor. By the end, she was sitting on the floor, her back against the wall and her head bent over between her knees, crying. It was one of those silent cries—I'm not sure whether the nun on the other end could even tell.

Finally, the conversation was over, but Mother continued to sit there for several minutes, weeping silently. Eventually, she got up and, after composing herself, told me what the conversation had been about, that I would not be going to Camden Park. I don't remember feeling pained by the exclusion nearly so much as I was shaken and hurt by seeing my mother, unable to protect one of her children from abuse, cry as she did that day.

Mother and Daddy both told me stories of racial abuses and indignities suffered as children and as adults. But they told me other stories as well.

One that sticks in my mind is of how a couple of Daddy's Catholic colleagues at the Ashland prison decided that they were going to get their new colleague into the Holy Family chapter of the Knights of Columbus. The K. of C. apparently had long been known as unwelcoming to blacks. But very shortly, with these men's sponsorship, Daddy became a member of the Holy Family chapter. It may have been that the door was unlocked and just needed to be pushed on. But those men took the initiative to do it.

And then there was Mr. Graybeal.

Walter Graybeal was the reason our family had come to Ashland in the first place, and the reason we children ended up at Holy Family School. Daddy used to say that Graybeal, in effect, gave up his career so Daddy could have one. Mother, never one to deal in cheap grace, paid Graybeal and his wife, Eleanor, her ultimate compliment: "Those were *good* people."

Walter Graybeal was a lapsed Catholic who was raised in Lafayette, Indiana. He earned a degree from Indiana State University in Terre Haute and served in the U.S. Army during World War II. After the war, he came home and went to work in the federal prison system. He was the supervisor of education at the prison in Ashland in early 1954, and it was into his hands that the job application of a young veteran from Dayton, Texas, fell. It was he who decided to hire that young veteran, Wilbert Wycliff.

BEFORE THE BYLINE DON WYCLIFF

Daddy said it was quite evident to him when he showed up to work on that first day in June 1954 that nobody was expecting the new hire to be a black man. Mother said Graybeal later told her that he had overlooked the part of the application that identified Daddy as a graduate of the "Texas State University for Negroes," now Texas Southern University. But it wouldn't have mattered to him anyway, he said. Graybeal apparently was the kind of guy who, when he made up his mind, went with it and fought for his decisions. And he made up his mind that Wilbert Wycliff was the man for the open teaching job in his department.

Daddy recalled a long conversation with Graybeal on one of his first days on the job, during which Graybeal bared his soul on the subject of race. "He said he didn't feel comfortable with the idea of blacks and whites marrying," Daddy recalled. "Since I wasn't looking to get married, that wasn't going to be a problem."

After it became clear that Daddy and his new boss were a good fit, Graybeal began driving him around Ashland to look at housing and schools. They visited Booker T. Washington, the black school, and while Daddy liked the people at the school, the condition of the place was an old, familiar story to him: The building was decrepit, and the books and equipment were worn and cast off from the white schools. He wanted something better for his kids.

And that was how we ended up at Holy Family.

After we left Ashland, Daddy and Graybeal remained friends and kept in close touch. After Daddy retired from prison work and was ordained a permanent deacon of the Catholic Church, Graybeal, who by then was a widower living in San Antonio with his only child, a daughter, came to Dallas for Daddy's ordination. He died in 1981. "Mr. Graybeal" was always a revered figure in our household.

So was Grace Jamison. We children grew up hearing Mother speak of "Mrs. Jamison," the white woman in Dayton for whom she had worked in her youth. It wasn't until I was well into adulthood that I learned anything about her. I thought she had died back in the 1950s, but it turned out she lived until 1986.

Grace Borden Jamison was part of the family that owned the Borden dairy company. Her family originally was from the northeast—Connecticut or Rhode Island—but they came to Texas at some point, and Grace grew up on a ranch in the Lake Jackson area near the Gulf Coast. She met her husband, T.J. Jamison, a Dayton resident, when they both were undergraduates at Sam Houston State University. After college, they came to Dayton, her husband's home, to settle down and raise a family.

There were other such stories and other such figures. Mother used to talk about "Miss Pray," a woman who had known her mother when both lived in Louisiana and who made it a point during the Depression to bring food and usable clothing to Zilda and her family. Another woman, Mrs. Ernest, the wife of a postman, also looked out for the Broussards, having her husband drop off food along with the family's mail.

But such charity didn't run in just one direction. Daddy told of a white man who, again during the Depression, walked six miles one day from the nearby settlement of Kenefick to Grandpa's shop in downtown Dayton.

Besides blacksmithing, Grandpa operated a gristmill at his shop at that time, grinding corn into meal for customers in return for a portion of the product. He would then sell meal to anyone who needed it.

When the man from Kenefick showed up, Grandpa was away, and Daddy was managing the shop. The man had no money, but he told Daddy he would return the next week and pay him if he would let him have ten pounds of cornmeal—30 cents worth—on credit. Daddy agreed to do so.

The man took the sack of cornmeal and started to leave. Then he stopped, turned around and said, "You know, there are some good colored people in this world. And when we get to heaven, we're gonna make a place for 'em."

I guess that was supposed to satisfy his sense of duty to be polite while preserving his sense of superiority as a white man.

So race has always been more complicated—at least in our family and at the personal level—than just oppression and black-white antagonism. Even so, all the personal courage and decency of people like Mr. Graybeal and Mrs. Jamison couldn't change the fact that race was, most often, about systematic institutional inequality, enforced by fundamentally brutal, terroristic means.

We had examples of this in our own family, too. My uncle Frank, the one who taught me how to make bows and arrows and who was my favorite uncle, told of being beaten for no reason by two Houston police officers. Frank, who loved to dress well, was working at the time at the Port of Houston, doing some sort of manual labor. He had finished his work week and gone home to where he was living in Houston, bathed, changed into nice clothes and was on his way to eat at a restaurant in Third Ward.

Just as he was putting his hand on the doorknob of the restaurant, he said he was grabbed from behind by two cops. Without explanation, they took him to a nearby woods and thrashed him.

No explanation. No recourse.

CHAPTER 6
SUMMERTIME

Beginning our first year in Ashland, we established a pattern: When June arrived and summer vacation began, the older kids in the family went "home" to Texas. The summer of 1955, Grandma, Grandpa and Uncle Sam Wickliff drove up to visit us and then returned to Dayton with Francois, Karen and me in the car with them. We stayed until just before the start of the next school year in September.

I loved those summers in the country. They provided me with dozens of moments and memories that live on in my mind, along with life lessons that have shaped and guided me through the decades. At the center of these adventures were five personalities: Grandma and Grandpa; Aunt Willie B. Smith, Grandma's older sister; Rosa Bryant—"Miss Rosie"—Parrain's wife and, for a good part of my youth, his widow; and Freddie Joe Ford, a boy Francois' age who lived several dozen yards up the road from Grandma and Grandpa in a house he shared with his grandmother and an older cousin. These were the people who filled our daily lives, sharing their work, their stories, their knowledge, their time with us.

In the early years, it was Grandma who loomed largest in our lives. She had been a schoolteacher, teaching fourth grade at Colbert Elementary School, when we left Dayton and moved to Ashland. But she fell

BEFORE THE BYLINE DON WYCLIFF

seriously ill shortly after our departure. In early 1955, I recall, Mother and Daddy pulled Francois, Karen and me out of school for a few days so the entire family could rush back to Dayton to see Grandma. Her illness was diabetes, far more difficult to control in those days than it is now. She didn't die, but she was left disabled. She took to walking with a cane and, when she was around home, she moved about most of the time in a wheelchair.

After her health crisis, Grandma retired from teaching. She mostly kept house, cooking and cleaning. When we came for the summers, she pressed us into service on both of those chores. She also had us help with her work as treasurer of Pleasant Hill Baptist Church. We would count the money from the collection plates and wrap the coins in paper tubes that Grandma or Grandpa would deposit into the church's account at the Dayton State Bank downtown. Grandma had an adding machine that I always wished I could use, but never got to.

Grandma was a good but not a great cook—certainly not as good, I thought, as Mother was. But at the end of every meal, Grandpa would lean back in his chair and pronounce his judgment, which never varied: "Mighty nice. Migh-tee nice!"

In the early years, Grandma still kept chickens. We kids would go and fetch the eggs from the chickenhouse, being careful to watch for snakes, which also fancied hen's eggs. Grandma would occasionally kill a chicken to cook. She would catch whatever unlucky bird she had set her eye on, holding it initially by its feet in her left hand. Then she would grab the chicken's neck with her right hand, whirl it around several times, and let it go. The poor bird would go flopping about for a while before falling dead. Grandma would then chop off the head, drain the blood, dump the body in boiling water, pluck the feathers, gut the bird, and cut it up. I don't recall ever wanting to wring a chicken's neck.

The house on the hillside was surrounded by pecan, black walnut and fig trees. The pecans ripened and fell in the fall, so we were never around to help harvest them. It was pretty much the same with the walnuts, although it was so hard to crack and pick the meat out of those that they generally went unharvested by anybody. But the fig trees bore abundantly and at just the right time for us to help gather them. Two or three days each week, we would go out and fill buckets with ripe figs, which Grandma would preserve. Snakes sometimes were a factor in this activity, too. I have a vivid memory of the day Francois used Grandpa's shotgun to blow a huge, hissing snake to pieces after it took up residence in the biggest of the fig trees. I don't know whether the snake was venomous or not, but we didn't consider that important. We were terrified of them all.

Grandma would take our figs, wash them, put them into big, iron kettles on her stovetop, and add sugar. Lots of it. She would boil the mixture for hours, until the fruit was soft and the juice syrupy. Then we would put it into Mason jars that had been carefully scalded and sterilized, and seal them tightly with a two-part lid, a flat top with a rubber seal around the outer edge, and a threaded collar that would hold the top in place. We would always return to Ashland in the fall with a generous supply of preserved figs, which we enjoyed eating with biscuits. Many were the times when I made a meal of just fig preserves and biscuits.

There were also a few peach and pear trees on the property, and Grandma would preserve those fruits as well. One summer, she decided to show us how to make peach brandy. The result was a very strong alcoholic beverage, which Grandma called "peach Molly darlin'."

One of the things I liked most about Grandma was her endless supply of rhymes and aphorisms and expressions, which she must have learned either by reading or by listening to old folks when she was young. Among my favorites was this playful one:

BEFORE THE BYLINE DON WYCLIFF

"Your eyes may shine,
And your teeth may grit,
But none of my [fill in the blank]
Shall you git!"

There was one she used to recite when bedtime approached:

"To bed, to bed," said Sleepyhead
"No, wait a while," said Slow.
"Put on the pot," said Pusslegut,
"Let's eat before we go!"

The addition of an ingredient that made a dish more tasty or an activity more enjoyable would elicit, "That makes the cheese more binding." And there was a word that I never heard except from Grandma and other old black folks: "drylongso." It was used mainly in reference to food, and it seemed to mean plain, simple, unadorned, unspiced. "You can eat it just drylongso."

As I grew older and stronger, I began to spend less time with Grandma and more with Grandpa. He was always up early, dressed in his workday uniform of blue denim overalls, white tee shirt and long-sleeved work shirt. Before breakfast, he would take a turn around the twelve-acre field behind the house, checking on his crops, watching for where raccoons or other varmints might have invaded to feast on his sweet potatoes, his peas and beans, his watermelons or his Irish potatoes. (Grandpa always called them Irish potatoes, to distinguish them from sweet potatoes or yams. But he pronounced the word "Irish" as "osh." It was only after I was fully grown and was reading one day about the Irish potato famine that I had an epiphany and realized that what Grandpa called "osh potatoes" were "Irish potatoes.")

Almost all of Grandpa's crops were already in the ground and sprouting by the time we arrived in June. The only crop I recall helping to plant was sweet potatoes. That involved taking a piece of the potato vine, laying it perpendicularly atop a furrow, and, with a stick, pushing the vine into the ground, being careful to break it so that it could begin to absorb nutrients and grow.

The crop we kids valued the most was watermelons. To be sure, we liked to eat them. It has been years since I tasted a watermelon as sweet and juicy as those Grandpa raised. But we also loved them because we could sell them. We would go periodically out into the field and harvest a batch—looking for the yellow spot on the dark green rind that indicated ripeness—load them onto the trailer attached to Grandpa's tractor, and drive down the dusty dirt roads, selling melons to people in the Lowoods community.

The melons varied in shape and size from round to oblong, from small to very large, several pounds. They were not the standard-sized things you get in supermarkets nowadays. And they were tastier. The smaller ones we'd sell for a quarter ("two bits," Grandpa called it); the bigger ones for maybe two dollars. And we got to keep the money!

After breakfast, Grandpa would head off to his blacksmith shop downtown. In later years, I would go with him. But in the early years, I stayed at home and, along with Francois and Karen, helped Grandma around the farm. Francois and I were responsible for, among other things, releasing the sheep—Grandpa always had twenty to thirty head—from the pen behind the house where they spent nights into a pasture across the road in front of the house. It was then that I learned how dumb sheep could be. The slightest change in the appearance of the pathway from pen to pasture could stop them, alarm them, render them confused. I recall once some engine oil was spilled in front of the pasture gate. It left a black spot three or four feet in diameter. The next day, when the sheep reached that point, they stopped, baffled. Finally, one of them decided to leap over the black spot. All the rest did the same. Silly creatures.

BEFORE THE BYLINE DON WYCLIFF

Another of Grandma's favorite expressions was "all work and no play makes Jack a dull boy." Jill, too. So we had plenty of time for play.

In those days, thanks to television, we were all into cowboys. I—and I know Karen felt the same—always wanted to have a horse with a fancy saddle and be able to ride the range, shooting bad guys with six-guns. Since we didn't have real horses, we made do with sticks and our imaginations: stick horses.

A particular kind of bush, a weed, grew in abundance around our grandparents' house in those days, mainly in the drainage ditches along the roadsides. The plant had a green stalk that could reach six or seven feet and was topped by wispy leaves near the top. We would cut off the stalk at the bottom, strip off the leaves so that our "horse" had just the right amount of tail, put it between our legs, and go ripping and running down the road, through the fields, everywhere, riding our stick horses.

The gun part was a bit more difficult. Our Christmas wish lists always included toy six-guns—cap pistols. They were cheaply made, shiny, and quickly broken—except for Karen's Dale Evans model, which lasted and lasted until, she swears, it was stolen in Ashland by Apple Girl.

One of our first orders of business each summer was to scour the property to find a vine on which we could swing over a gully or ravine. When we found a good one, we would cut it off close to the ground and return to it often. With a good running start, a kid could propel himself or herself a good ten to twenty feet into the air above the ground. We loved that thrill.

We also played jacks, a game that's great for developing manual dexterity. It's hard for me now, with my arthritic hands, to believe I once could pick up all ten jacks during the time it took for that little red rubber ball to bounce once and fall back into my hand.

* * *

I have never seen a man who worked harder than Grandpa. And as I grew older, I began to work with him during those Texas summers. The last couple of summers of his life, which were the last couple of summers of high school for me, Grandpa felt confident enough in my strength and my abilities to let me do jobs at the shop for pay. There was a fellow who had a contract to mow the grass on the sides of the highways in the area; he used to bring dull blades to Grandpa to be sharpened. I did some of that work, which required heating the blades in the forge and beating out the edges until they were thin and sharp. I also did a little welding. But some tasks—sharpening plow points, for example—were too sophisticated for me.

Grandpa's confident assertion—"I'll fix it or I'll fix it so nobody else can fix it"—sometimes led to attempts to work on things that, strictly speaking, weren't within a blacksmith's area of competence. I shudder sometimes when I think of the day someone brought a power lawn mower to the shop and asked whether Grandpa could make it work. He and I fiddled with the thing for an hour or more, trying to figure out how to get it started. We turned it every which way but loose, looking for the problem. Finally, we gave up.

Some time later, I saw a fellow with a similar mower start his: It required folding out a little arm atop the engine, cranking it around several times, then refolding the arm. When the arm snapped into place, the engine roared to life. Thank God neither Grandpa nor I had thought to try that. We both would have lost hands, arms, or maybe our lives.

There was a rhythm to our summers, the rhythm of agriculture. Early on, the sheep had to be sheared, and the cattle had to be branded. Grandpa was good at shearing. He managed to snip the wool off the animals without nicking them. I was not so good. I suspect every sheep in the flock recoiled in terror when they saw me with a pair of shears in my hand. After the shearing was done, we would bundle up the wool and, one day toward the end of the summer, drive into Houston to sell it to a dealer.

Later in the summer, as the grasses grew long and the crops matured, we would mow lots and fields and transport the hay back to the barn to feed the livestock in the coming winter. Every summer, it seemed, Grandpa would have rigged up a new gadget or device to lighten the load and save some labor. Sometimes they worked; sometimes they seemed to me more trouble than they were worth.

Our machinery, especially the little Allis-Chalmers tractor, was never as reliable as it needed to be. One summer, an axle snapped, putting the tractor out of action for a couple of crucial weeks. Another time, the mower got fouled up, and Grandpa had to send away for a part, which also took weeks.

One of the most valuable life lessons I learned came on a day when Grandpa and I were out in the field, working on some problem afflicting the tractor. A man I had never met before—a tall, light-skinned fellow with a strong French Creole accent—had come out to talk to Grandpa about something, and he was standing about as we worked.

At some point, Grandpa asked me a question to which I replied, "Yes."

The Creole fellow jumped in, indignantly reprimanding me. "Boy, you can't say 'Yes, sir'?" he huffed.

I stood there, befuddled by his interruption, his tone of voice, and his question. But Grandpa came to my rescue.

"Where he comes from," Grandpa said firmly, "they don't say 'Yes, sir' to nobody, young or old, black or white."

At that, the fellow stammered something that wasn't quite an apology and shut up.

I have always remembered what Grandpa said that day and have taken it as an obligation to live up to. I have tried to say "Yes, sir" only as an indication of genuine respect, not out of any sense of duty.

* * *

Besides a trip to the beach in Galveston, the highlight of our summer visits was always the nineteenth of June, emancipation day for black folks in Texas. It was on June 19, 1865, that Union troops reached Galveston and informed the slaves there that the Civil War was over and they were free. That knowledge had been kept from them until then by their former slavemasters.

Black folks throughout the state took the day off and celebrated their emancipation. In Dayton, there was a nineteenth of June parade downtown. I remember one year, Francois got to drive Grandpa's tractor in the parade. I looked forward to the day when I would be able to do that, but by the time I was old enough, the parade had been discontinued.

Grandpa always slaughtered a lamb and had it barbecued for the nineteenth. I was fascinated by the slaughter, as I was by everything Grandpa did. He would select a lamb—not a newborn but one six months to a year old—and hang it by the heels of its hind legs from a rafter in the garage. Then, using the long blade of the pocket knife he always carried and honed carefully for days in advance, he would slit the animal's throat. As its blood drained into a bucket, the sacrificial lamb and the rest of the flock performed a poignant kind of call-and-response. The dying lamb would bleat, and the flock would bleat back in response. As much as I enjoyed barbecue, I couldn't help but feel sad listening to this death song.

Once the lamb had bled out, Grandpa would cut away the skin and gut the animal, getting down to the meat. When the slaughter was completed, he would take the meat to a fellow in Liberty to be barbecued. A day or two later, on the nineteenth, the deliciously browned and fragrant result would return to us, ready for eating.

Parrain also barbecued for the nineteenth, but he always barbecued a goat. And he did the whole business himself, right down to cooking the meat over a pit dug into the ground. He used fence wire as his grill.

* * *

It was Grandpa who taught me to drive, putting me behind the wheel of their Chevy on those dusty back roads. He was an easy, gentle teacher, and I was a pretty apt student. Besides learning to manipulate the car skillfully and safely, I learned some of the etiquette involved in being a car owner in a time and place where many people were not so privileged.

There was a couple who lived just down the road from Grandma's and Grandpa's place. Their names were Lonnie and Blondena Roberts. Lonnie was generally known by his nickname, Dirty Buddy. I never learned the origin of that name and, honestly, never thought to ask. Dirty Buddy was severely disabled, whether as a result of an accident or a birth defect, I never knew. He had a badly deformed arm—the left one, I think—and a bad leg that left him with a gimpy, twisted walk. Blondena was extremely overweight. Nevertheless, they would trudge together to and from downtown Dayton, to shop, visit the doctor, or transact other business.

I learned never to pass by Dirty Buddy and Blondena without offering them a ride, which they would always gratefully accept. They also accepted the armadillos—"Hoover hogs," Grandma called them—that we occasionally would shoot. Armadillos were pretty harmless creatures and there was no real need to kill them, but at the time, I didn't think about that.

One form of recreation during our summers was "going visiting." We would pile into the car with Grandma and Grandpa and drive to Liberty, Ames, Moss Bluff, Hardin or one of the other nearby towns and drop in to visit with friends or relatives. It seemed that every place we went, we would meet some new person, and Grandpa would tell us, "That's your kinfolks." I most often had no sense of how they were kin to us, but I took Grandpa at his word.

To this day, when I hear the old Drifters' recording, "There Goes My Baby," I think of one of those summer-evening trips out to Hardin to visit a friend of Grandma's named Lellar, last name unknown to me. The sun was sinking toward the western horizon behind us. The land had an orange-reddish glow. The trees were tall and still. The air was hot and humid. The sand on the road was deep. And the Drifters sang, "Movin'on, down the line," just as we were moving down that old country road.

There was one aspect of our summers in Dayton that I *didn't* like: going to church with Grandma. Not that I disliked her church or the people or the services. On the contrary, I loved them all, although the services could have been briefer. But Grandma was a Baptist, and we were Catholics, and in those days Catholics were taught that it was a sin to go to a church other than a Catholic one. Not just a sin, but a mortal sin. And if you died with a mortal sin on your soul, you went to hell. No appeal. No leniency.

So every Sunday, as I would sit with Grandma and Grandpa in a pew at Pleasant Hill Baptist Church, I worried that I might die before I made it to confession and might, as a result, spend eternity in hell.

What utter foolishness! What a perverse thing to lay such a burden on a child!

* * *

At some point in the late 1950s, Aunt Willie retired from her government job in Washington, DC, and came back to Dayton to live with Ida and Sprig. She moved into a bedroom on the north side of the house.

BEFORE THE BYLINE DON WYCLIFF

For some reason, Grandma and Aunt Willie took to calling each other "Molly." It never was clear to me why, but I think it stemmed from a mutual affection for the Molly Goldberg show on TV.

Aunt Willie is most memorable to me as the passionate keeper of the household's three dogs: Boy, Missy and Cindy. Missy and Cindy were mother and daughter; Boy was Cindy's father, but also, I believe, the father of a litter of her children. In those days, I don't think folks bothered much with spaying and neutering.

The dogs were a mixture of breeds—chow and something else. They had beautiful black and brown coats. But their good looks and pleasant names belied their personalities. They were ferocious.

They were kept in the yard by a chain-link fence. Once or twice, I saw some hapless visitor get terrified out of his wits when he rested an arm atop the fence and the three dogs, fangs bared and growling like Cerberus, came tearing out from beneath the house to attack the intruder. Once or twice, if I recall correctly, they actually hurt someone who wasn't aware of their existence or their ferocity. And for years after they had died, visitors to "Miss Ida's house" would ask, "Y'all still have those dogs?"

The dogs seemed comfortable and well-behaved with us children. Grandma, Grandpa and Aunt Willie used to brag that the dogs liked us. But I, for one, never really felt at ease in their presence and was always on my guard.

Aunt Willie became boon companions with Miss Rosie. They would walk their dogs together two or three times a day—Aunt Willie's three and Miss Rosie's one. Walking sticks in hand and straw hats on their heads, they would traverse the roads and fields around the homestead, and Aunt Willie would return and recite at great length her observations about the conditions of fences, evidence of wildlife presences and anything else that seemed remotely unusual. Had she lived in another time and place, Aunt Willie would have been a true griot.

Miss Rosie, for her part, was mostly silent, a posture I suspect she learned during forty years of marriage to William Bryant, "Parrain".

Rosa Bryant has to have been one of the meekest persons ever to walk the earth, but she did not, the Sermon on the Mount notwithstanding, inherit it. She did, however, outlive her husband, which may have been just as good.

Born December 11, 1883, in Camilla Hill, Texas, she was the daughter of a minister, W.M. McKenzie, and a mother whose name I have been unable to discover. She married Parrain in 1920 and spent the next four decades as his wife, shuttling with him between Dayton and the little community of Five Mile Settlement as his temperament dictated. He died in October 1960, leaving her a widow.

Theirs was, to all outward appearances, an old-fashioned marriage in which the woman served and the man dominated. "Rosie!" Parrain used to bark when he wanted her attention. She always responded quickly and without complaint.

Like many older black folks at that time, Miss Rosie dipped snuff. She kept a small garden behind her house. And every day, toward evening, she could be heard singing hymns alone in her house.

Miss Rosie died in July 1983. She was ninety-nine years old.

* * *

And then there was Freddie Joe. Freddie Joseph Ford was the first kid I ever knew who didn't have a dad in his home. He didn't have a mother, either, but it was the absence of a dad that made him stand out in my mind. His grandmother, Bessie Ford, was his guardian, rearing him and an older cousin because their own parents couldn't or wouldn't.

I can't remember now who Freddie Joe's parents were, or whether it was his mother or his father who was Miss Bessie's child. But I do know two things: He clearly suffered from the lack of a father or father-figure, and he loved it when summer came because it meant that the Wycliff kids would be coming "home" and he would have friends to play with.

Tall, foul-mouthed and obsessed with sex, Freddie Joe seemed beyond adult control from the first time I ever met him. I'll never forget the day Miss Bessie, his grandmother and guardian, shouted to him as he walked down the road away from home, "Where you going, Fred Joe?"

"To hell if I don't change my ways!" he shouted back, never breaking stride.

He had a litany of dirty doggerels. One example:

Monkey and the baboon playing in the grass.
The monkey stuck his finger up the baboon's ass.
The baboon said, 'Well bless my soul.
Get your finger out of my asshole.'

Freddy Joe had a skinny little black dog that he named "Black Gal." He had a way of saying her name so that it sounded like an obscenity.

The physical object of Freddie Joe's most ardent desire was a young woman from the neighborhood, Alice Faye Prater. I understood why: She was very pretty.

Then, one summer after I got into high school, we went home to Texas, and Alice Faye wasn't a girl anymore. She was a young woman with a baby.

I recall a day—I must have been about twelve—when we all went out into the woods together—Francois, Freddie Joe and I (I always liked to be with the big boys). There, Freddie Joe gave a demonstration of his prowess at masturbation. He bragged that he did it often, which probably explained why his performance at that moment was rather weak.

One of his chores was to split wood for Miss Bessie to burn in her wood stove to cook and to heat water to do laundry for white folks. She always seemed at her wits' end trying to get Freddie Joe to perform this duty—or any other, for that matter.

"Fred Joe!" she would scream. "I ain't gon' tell you again ..." The first two words came out sounding almost Germanic: "Eingah ..."

When she became truly frustrated, she would deliver a classic threat: "I'll salivate you!"

I don't remember the last time I saw Freddie Joe. It probably was the summer Francois graduated from high school. I don't know what happened to him after that.

BEFORE THE BYLINE DON WYCLIFF

IMAGES FROM MY ROOTS

These photographs capture some of the people and moments that shaped my story. Some I knew personally, others lived generations before me, but all reflect the roots from which my journey and this book grew.

AMANDA GIBBS, Don's great-great-grandmother

NAPOLEON "PAUL" BROUSSARD, "Papa," father of Emily Broussard Wycliff, grandfather of Don Wycliff.

BEFORE THE BYLINE DON WYCLIFF

LEANA "LIT" DAY, daughter of Isaiah Cates Day and Amanda Gibbs; born about 1868; mother of Willie B. Speights Smith and Ida Belle Brown Wycliff; grandmother of Wilbert Wycliff; great grandmother of Don Wycliff.

SYLVESTER "BIG PAPA" WYCLIFF, son of Michel Paul and Lucy Hunt Paul; born 1864 in Verdunville, Louisiana; changed his name sometime in the 1890s from Paul, his birth surname, to Wycliff; died Dec. 31, 1959; married Epheme Pradier in 1896; father of seven children; oldest was Socrates; grandfather of Wilbert Wycliff; great grandfather of Don Wycliff.

PORTRAIT OF THE WYCLIFF FAMILY OF AMES, TEXAS. Seated left to right: Sylvester (patriarch), daughters Stella, Madgalene, Frances, Epheme (matriarch). Standing left to right: Socrates, Plato, Edward "Timme", Michael "Sam."

SOCRATES "SPRIG" WYCLIFF, husband of Ida, father of Wilbert, grandfather of Don Wycliff.

SOCRATES, THE BUSINESSMAN, in front of his blacksmith shop in downtown Dayton.

WILBERT WYCLIFF in Army uniform.

WILBERT WYCLIFF AND TWO BUDDIES in Rome during World War II.

BEFORE THE BYLINE DON WYCLIFF

WILBERT AND EMILY WYCLIFF WITH BABY FRANCOIS in Washington, D.C., in August 1943 before Wilbert's deployment to Italy.

EMILY BROUSSARD WYCLIFF as a young woman.

LEFT TO RIGHT: DON, KAREN, FRANCOIS as kids.

WYCLIFF FAMILY ON THE ROAD in Kentucky.

BEFORE THE BYLINE DON WYCLIFF

WYCLIFF CHILDREN IN PORTRAIT. Standing left to right: Don, Francois, Karen, Chris. In front, left to right: Ida, Joy.

FAMILY WITH GRANDMA IDA WYCLIFF visiting Brother Thaddeus (Francois) at Mt. Alverno Monastery in Cincinnati in 1963.

DON WYCLIFF on First Communion Day, May 8, 1955.

WYCLIFF FAMILY in front of Central Avenue house on the morning of May 8, 1955, Don's First Communion Day.

DON AND PARENTS at his Notre Dame graduation, June 1969.

BEFORE THE BYLINE DON WYCLIFF

THE CONGREGATION OF ST. JOSEPH the Worker Catholic Church in Dayton, around 1955.

WILBERT WYCLIFF STANDS IN FRONT OF A MURAL inside the new Dayton Civic Center on dedication day in January 2010. The mural depicts his father, Socrates, working on a wagon wheel (he was a blacksmith and wheelwright).

THE WYCLIFF HOMESTEAD. It stood from roughly 1917 until 2019, the year after Wilbert died.

CHAPTER 7

WESTWARD HO!

In 1960, while Mother and Daddy were in the midst of expanding our house on Hilton Avenue in Ashland, Daddy got word that he was being promoted and transferred. He was to become Assistant Supervisor of Education at the Federal Correctional Institution in Englewood, Colorado.

As soon as we children were told about the impending move, I became excited. Just the name of the new state—Colorado—stirred me. One of those blue-backed biographies that I had read had been about Zebulon Pike, the explorer after whom Pike's Peak was named. There would be mountains with snow on them all year round. There probably would be cowboys and cattle drives and all kinds of exciting adventures to be had.

I was not without regret at the prospect of leaving Ashland. We would be leaving friends—the Foleys, and my classmates at Holy Family. I didn't at that time fully appreciate what those Ashland years had done for us as a family and for me as an individual. They had launched us in a completely different direction from the one we were going in in Dayton. We were headed upward, taking flight.

The move to Denver was much less of an ordeal than the one from Dayton to Ashland had been six years earlier, but it wasn't carefree. In

BEFORE THE BYLINE DON WYCLIFF

1960, a moving van came and carried our belongings away. We were able to drive down to Texas to visit Grandma, Grandpa and Aunt Willie on the hillside in Dayton. On the way down, we stopped in Memphis and stayed overnight at the Lorraine Motel, the black hostelry where, eight years later, Dr. Martin Luther King Jr. would be assassinated. Black students at North Carolina A&T University had touched off the lunch counter sit-in movement in February of 1960, but it would be years still before we could stop at any place along our southern route, enter through the front door, sit down and dine.

After our Dayton visit, we headed north and west to Denver. Toward evening of our first day on the road, we stopped and had dinner at a restaurant in the black section of Amarillo, Texas. And later we stayed overnight in a motel, whether in New Mexico or Colorado, I don't remember.

What I do recall from that trip, and vividly, was our passage through the little town of Raton, New Mexico. Daddy had stopped the car at an intersection to wait for the traffic light to change. I looked out a window of our Chevy station wagon and saw, stepping off the curb, a young Hispanic girl of about my age, thirteen. I thought she was beautiful and I was immediately in love—or probably just in lust. I was all raging hormones in those days.

Our first several weeks in Denver, we stayed—all of us, two adults and seven children—in a single room of a big house on Emerson Street, near downtown Denver. The bathroom, which we shared with other tenants, was down a hallway. This place was a stopgap while Mother and Daddy shopped for and then bought a small, red-brick, ranch-style house in the Park Hill neighborhood of Denver. I don't know how Mother and Daddy found either place, but they obviously had already had plenty of practice at being resourceful in such matters.

My impression was that the Emerson Street house was owned by another family who lived there, the Cannons, although they may have been renters as well. The Cannons, like everybody else in the neighborhood, were black, and I cannot now remember how many were in the family. But those I do remember are imprinted indelibly on my mind. There was an older daughter, about my age or Karen's, and a little boy, Junior, who must have been about four or five. There was Mr. Cannon, a tall, slender man of about Daddy's age who worked somewhere at something that I'm not sure I ever knew, and Mrs. Cannon, a tall, portly woman who took care of the children and loved to go to the greyhound races.

Junior was memorable because his play consisted mainly of pretending that he was a dog. He would tie a rope around his neck as a leash and bark at people and otherwise mimic a dog. I recall hearing some grownup opine that he probably did this in an effort to win attention and favor from his mother, who spent so much time at the dog tracks. Sometime after we had left the Cannons' and moved into our own house, I recall hearing that Junior had almost killed himself. He tied one end of a rope around his neck and the other end to some stationary object on the family's front porch. Then he jumped off, almost strangling himself, before someone found and resuscitated him.

Mr. Cannon I remember mostly because of a line that he loved to repeat. "I'll go up as high as the next man," he would say, "as long as I can keep one foot on the ground." I don't remember the context in which he said this—it probably had something to do with manned space flight, which was being much talked about in those days, even though the first manned flight, by a Russian, would not actually happen until 1961. But he said it often enough during our time there that I've remembered it ever since. And he said it in that emphatic way that certain men have of saying something trite as if they are convinced it is profound.

Also living in the Cannon house that summer was a teenage girl who was older than I but younger than Francois. I don't remember her

BEFORE THE BYLINE DON WYCLIFF

first name or how she came to be part of the Cannon household, but I do recall her last name—Mixon—and that she had ... breasts! She was pretty, brown-skinned and she obviously rang Francois' bell. We spent a lot of time during our sojourn on Emerson jumping rope in the small front yard, and young Miss Mixon was a lovely sight to behold when she jumped. It was a good time to be an adolescent boy.

Sometime before that summer, I had begun to associate significant periods and episodes in my life with music—songs that were popular at the particular moment. When I think of our Dayton years, for example, I think of a bawdy tune that must have been popular on black radio then, and which Karen and I memorized and used to delight in singing. The key lines went:

> *I'm gonna load my pistol,*
> *Gonna sharpen my knife.*
> *I'm gonna get. that. man. that. stole. my. wife.*
> *Booty, man! Booty!*

The Ashland years I mainly associate with Elvis Presley, but there also were Lloyd Price ("Personality" and "Stagger Lee"), the Fleetwoods ("Mister Blue," "Come Softly, To Me"), Laverne Baker ("Jim Dandy to the Rescue") and a group called the Browns, whose song "The Three Bells" seemed to play non-stop while it was popular. The Drifters had a raft of great hits, as did the Platters, still one of my all-time favorite groups.

But no musical memory compares with those from the summer of 1960. That was the summer of Roy Orbison's "Only the Lonely," Elvis Presley's "It's Now or Never," and Brenda Lee's "I Want to Be Wanted." (Already back then, I had a weakness for romantic ballads, generally the more saccharine the better.) It was the summer of Jimmy Jones's "Good Timing" and "Handy Man," and Brook Benton's and Dinah Washington's "Baby, You've Got What It Takes," and "A Rockin' Good Way." It was the summer of Marty Robbins's classic, "El Paso," and Marv Johnson's "You've Got What It Takes."

During our month or more on Emerson, we listened to those songs again and again on the radio and tried to stay sane. After Mother and Daddy completed the purchase of our house, we moved from the Cannons' to 2974 Dahlia Street in Park Hill on the east side of Denver. Like all the houses we ever had, it was too small for our family. This house had been built with two bedrooms, one of which was Mother's and Daddy's, and the other of which was the girls'. At some point, the garage had been turned into a third bedroom, which was occupied by the boys—Francois, Chris and me.

At some point during our three years in Denver, Mother's aunt, Sister Mary Ambrose—formerly Amanda Darby—came to visit. She was always an honored guest in our house, so we ate especially well during her visit. That meant lots of fried chicken, her favorite. But that pleasure came at a price: We boys had to surrender our room for the duration of her visit. And since in those days nuns always traveled with a companion, it meant two additional competitors for the one bathroom in the household.

Our house was three doors from the north end of our block. Our next-door neighbors to the north were the Harrises, a black family of mother, father and at least three children, including two daughters who were about Chris's and Karen's ages. And next to them, at the end of the block, was a white family, the Gadarowskis. Mr. Gadarowski was a tall, slender man who took long walks through the neighborhood and could always be counted on to greet you with a hearty "Top of the morning to you!" There were several Gadarowski children, but I remember only two of them, little blond boys who were about Chris's and Ida's ages and who used to carry on like the Katzenjammer Kids in the comic strip. I don't remember any of our neighbors to the south.

BEFORE THE BYLINE DON WYCLIFF

Park Hill was still a relatively young neighborhood in those days. It stretched eastward from Colorado Boulevard to Stapleton Airport. The streets ran in alphabetical order, with two streets each starting with each letter of the alphabet. Houses in Park Hill grew increasingly large and fancy the deeper into the alphabet and the closer to the airport you went. I was too young to realize it then, but our arrival was probably the start of the turnover of the neighborhood from white people to black. I don't know where the whites moved, but Park Hill was a step up for us. Not just to home ownership—we had owned the Hilton Avenue house in Ashland—but to a *brick* house in a cookie-cutter middle-class neighborhood with nice streets and middle-class amenities. I don't think I ever got over the existence in our house of a little compartment into which a milkman would place bottles or cartons of milk in the morning, and we could simply open the inner door to bring them into the kitchen.

I used to stand in our backyard and watch the bellies of planes that had just taken off from Stapleton and were climbing high into the sky. Oddly, it never occurred to me then to want to fly on one of those planes. Air travel seemed especially dangerous and, like Mr. Cannon, I always wanted to keep at least one foot on the ground.

Our house was across the street from a public elementary school, Stedman, where Joy would go to kindergarten. It was about a block south of Cure d'Ars Church, where we would go to Mass, and Cure d'Ars School, where Karen, Chris, Ida and I would go to school. It was about a mile north of Machebeuf High School, where I would spend my first two years of high school. However, when we moved into our house, Machebeuf didn't yet have a senior class, so Francois, who was a senior, had to take a bus to downtown Denver each day to attend Cathedral High School.

Named for the sainted French priest Jean Vianney, Cure d'Ars—inevitably, the French pronunciation (cue-ray-dar) gave way to an Americanized one (cure-dee-ars)—seemed as new and disorienting to me in its way as Holy Family had been when we first arrived in Ashland. The kids at Cure d'Ars seemed more mature and worldly, which was only to be expected since Denver was a big city and Ashland was a small and relatively unsophisticated town in Appalachia.

But the biggest change for me was that boys and girls attended classes together at Cure d'Ars. That meant I was exposed daily not just to Nick Tolve, Greg Beringer, Gary Arroyo, John Pagliasotti and other boys, but also to Michelle Bailey, Kathy Dorchinez, Pat Hubbard (the only other black student in my class), Sharon Paul. Girls, girls, girls, with their developing bosoms straining against the buttons of their white uniform blouses and their developing hips showing under their green and white checked skirts. My hormones raged even more.

Unlike Holy Family, Cure d'Ars had a football team for seventh and eighth graders, and I allowed myself to be lured into playing. I hated it. Basically, I just didn't like hurling my body at others or having others hurl their bodies at me. But more particularly, the field next to the school where we practiced and sometimes played games was painful to play on. It had formerly been a waste dump of some sort. There was no grass, just soil, hard-packed and with a thin layer of dust on top. The soil was impregnated with briars, shards of broken glass and other hazardous stuff. I hated falling on that ground, but I did it a lot during that one season of football. I remember only a few of my teammates. There was Danny Miller, a team leader who was unique among us eighth graders because he owned a Vespa motor scooter, which he rode to school. And there was Gary Arroyo, a tall Hispanic kid who seemed all hard muscle and who loved to hurl himself at opposing players, both in practice and in games, with an abandon that I couldn't match. I don't think I ever was hit as hard as I was by Arroyo. Our coach was Jim Bowen, a tall, handsome young guy who made us run laps every day.

Cure d'Ars also had a basketball team, and that I enjoyed much more. Already in eighth grade, I was six feet tall and was learning to jump well. Height alone isn't an advantage, though, unless you've got the heft to handle yourself under the basket with other big guys. Sadly, I never had that heft, even through high school. But in eighth grade, I was proud just to be the only player on the team who could touch the basketball rim. I also had begun to develop an ability to block other players' shots.

I don't remember much about our basketball season. The one thing I do remember is that we once played a game against an all-black team from an inner-city school. One of the other team's guards was a kid named Gabe, and I had a sense that my teammates—all of them white, of course—took a disturbing and—I thought—racially tinged delight in laughing about his name.

Cure d'Ars was staffed mainly by the Sisters of the Precious Blood, a Dayton, Ohio-based order whose members dressed in gray habits topped off with black veils. The principal was Sister Carmencita. My eighth-grade teacher was Sister Madonna, who was tall and, I thought, very pretty. I developed an enormous crush on her. Many years later, while I was working in Dayton, I paid a visit to the motherhouse of the Precious Blood sisters. I had a nice visit with Sister Carmencita, who remembered me. I asked about Sister Madonna, and Sister Carmencita told me that Madonna had "left the community." I assumed that meant she had gotten married, and I wondered who the lucky guy was.

At Holy Family, I, and then Karen, and then Chris, had developed a facility for spelling. We became regular contestants in the school spelling bee and then the city's. Somehow, my reputation as a good speller preceded me to Cure d'Ars, and Sister Madonna decided I potentially could be a good representative of the school in the Denver spelling bee. That led to one of the things I liked least: sitting in a small room practicing spelling words while my classmates enjoyed recess outdoors.

In the end, I was good, but not good enough to get beyond the first round in the city bee. Karen did better than I, and Chris later did better than either of us. He made it to the Colorado state contest and, after we moved to Indiana, to that state contest as well.

I began to grow much more worldly-wise while I was at Cure d'Ars, even if I didn't always realize it. I recall one day during football season, we were running our laps before getting down to practice. I happened to be running along next to two of my teammates, and one of them was telling the other about watching as a friend of his had sex with a girl. As he described it, the coupling took place where the girl worked. "At first she fought some," he said, "but after a while she stopped." Only much later did I realize I had heard a description of a rape.

At Cure d'Ars was the first time I ever saw an American president, John F. Kennedy. He wasn't president yet when I saw him. It was the fall of 1960, and he was running for the office against Vice President Richard Nixon. Because Kennedy was potentially the first Catholic president, his passing by our school during a Denver campaign stop was deemed important enough for us to witness.

The entire school population, I think, stood on the sidewalk in front of the church at the corner of Dahlia and 32nd Streets as Kennedy passed by on the way from the airport to downtown Denver. It was a brilliantly sunny day. He sat atop the back seat of a convertible and waved to us as the car drove slowly past. I recall being struck by how red his hair was and how big his smile was. He really was a very handsome man.

I'm sure I didn't understand it then—I thought all white people were just white people—but I knew I had witnessed something special and different when, at a program in connection with our eighth-grade graduation, the father of one of my classmates, Hilda Sanchez, came with his mariachi band to play for our class. Until that performance, I had known nothing of Mexican music. But it was beautiful, and Hilda's father made his violin sing!

BEFORE THE BYLINE DON WYCLIFF

I graduated from eighth grade at Cure d'Ars in June 1961, at the same time Francois graduated from high school at Cathedral. Mother's brother, Uncle Simon, and our cousin Lillie Ruth Brown came up from Texas for Francois' graduation. What a good time we had! We still have old silent home movies of Simon clowning around while we all mowed the lawn and trimmed the shrubbery at our house. I don't think I ever saw Simon alive after that visit. He died in Seattle in December 1980 after a fairly dissipated life. He was only 47.

The summer of 1961, we spent, as usual, in Dayton. Grandma threw a big graduation party for Francois. All the kids who were his friends and would have been his classmates at Colbert High came. I will always remember one young man—everybody called him C.B.—jumping up to dance when Bobby Lewis's song "Tossin' and Turnin'" was played. That image has stayed in my mind ever since as the very picture of youthful joy and exuberance.

CHAPTER 8
LIVING A MILE HIGH

In the fall of 1961, Francois went off to Cincinnati as a postulant in the Brothers of the Poor of St. Francis. I went off to high school: Machebeuf High, named after the first Catholic bishop of Denver, Joseph Machebeuf. Once again, I was one of no more than a handful of black students in the school. Four of that handful were in my class: my Cure d'Ars classmate Patricia Hubbard; a boy named Lyman Hubbard, no relation to Pat; another girl named Norene Chambers, and me.

Machebeuf was staffed by the Sisters of Loretto, along with a sizable contingent of lay teachers. My Latin teacher, Don Landrum, was a layman, and so was my biology teacher, Ray Raclawski, and my algebra teacher, Robert Lankenau.

Mr. Lankenau was a Notre Dame graduate, the first I had ever met. He hailed from Brooklyn, and he used to delight in telling stories about the Dodgers of his youth, including one whose name I have never forgotten: Cookie Lavagetto. I don't know whether it was his fault or mine, but Mr. Lankenau's algebra class was where mathematics got hard for me. Worse than hard, actually. It became inscrutable, utterly opaque. Mr. Lankenau would stand at the blackboard scribbling out equations and explaining them in a tone that suggested this stuff was beyond simple, and I sat at my desk wondering what the hell all this was about. I have often thought that it would have been so much easier if somebody had told me at the beginning that mathematics is, essentially, a *language* for describing certain aspects of reality, rather than a set of puzzles about things that have no substance.

Mr. Raclawski wore a military-style crewcut and always spoke in a nasal, sing-songy tone. His most memorable phrase was "Typical freshman reaction," uttered when we freshmen behaved like ... well, freshmen, deriving amusement from some scatological remark or juvenile behavior. My most vivid memory from his class was when he operated on a frog, anesthetizing it, opening it up and letting us look at the still-beating heart and other organs. I'm pretty sure the patient did not survive that operation.

Mr. Landrum was probably my favorite teacher that freshman year. I found I liked Latin, and I liked the way he taught. If you asked him a question, he would either answer it right away or write himself a note to look up the answer, and he never forgot to do so. He was gracious, approachable, but not familiar. I liked his somewhat formal style.

The principal was a nun, Sister Mary Thomasine. I don't remember much about her except that she seemed distant and quite formidable. I was astonished when I attended the fortieth-year reunion of my Machebeuf class in 2005 and met her, now sporting the civilian look that most nuns adopted after the Second Vatican Council and calling herself by her original name, Rosemary Wilcox. She seemed like a real person.

There was another formidable personality on the faculty, also. That was Father Michael Walsh, associate pastor of Blessed Sacrament Parish, to which Machebeuf was somehow attached, and a teacher of religion. Catholic religion, that is. We were seriously indoctrinated in those days.

I have two memories of Father Walsh, who spoke with a cultivated Irish accent. One day in class, trying to make a point, he challenged us to play that old game "telephone." One person whispers a secret to another, and each person passes it along. The idea is that the message becomes increasingly corrupted as it passes from one person to the next. I don't know what the message was when it started out. I know only that it could not have been what the last boy in the class announced when he was asked to tell what he had been told: "Father Walsh is the most undaunted man in the world."

My other memory of Father Walsh comes from that day each year when the boys and the girls would be separated so that each group could receive the special "talk"—about sex, of course. In the news at that time was the story of Christine Jorgenson, who had just undergone a sex-change operation in Sweden to become a woman. Asked what he thought about the case, Father Walsh responded, "Well, I suppose you could say he has neither a pole nor a hole."

I made a number of great friends at Machebeuf. Male friends. There were Michael Mussett, Ron Gilbert, Earl Strate ("Ubi" we nicknamed him, the Latin word for "where," because he was short). There were Bernie Paoli, Clem Firko (one of our teachers, Mr. Hart, insisted on calling him "Clement"), Bob Lovett, and probably my favorite buddy at the time, a guy named Robert "Bob" Hickey.

I guess you could say I had a man-crush on Hickey. He was very short—no more than five feet, I would guess—and he had some sort of problem with his eyelids. It seemed he was always straining to look at other people, not just because he was always looking upward, but also because his eyelids wouldn't open fully. I think that because of his height and his eye problem, Hickey felt himself something of an outsider, as I did because of my race. But we both loved basketball, and so we became fast friends.

We were on the junior varsity (JV) basketball team that year, along with Strate, Paoli, Lovett, Firko, and some others, freshmen and sophomores. Machebeuf had no gym of its own—we used Blessed Sacrament

BEFORE THE BYLINE DON WYCLIFF

School's gym to practice, and we played our home games on Sundays at the gym of the then brand-new George Washington High School, a public school. Mr. Hart was the JV coach, and he took what, in hindsight, I recognize was a very healthy attitude toward our games: He wanted to make sure everyone got a chance to play, whether we won or not. It was frustrating to me to be lifted from the game so that someone not as good as I could play, but that's what happened routinely. There was one game, however, in which Mr. Hart just let us off the leash—the first team, that is. I had an especially productive day rebounding, and one of the sophomores, a fellow named John Fortune, shot the lights out with his old-fashioned set shot. I went home from that game feeling utterly fulfilled.

One of my most vivid memories from that freshman year was of a walk home after basketball practice with two teammates, Fortune and Firko, who lived north of the school as I did. It was late January 1962, and already dark as we made our way homeward about 5 p.m. There was a light snowfall, and flakes were swirling about, illuminated by the glow from the streetlights.

Gene Chandler's classic tune "Duke of Earl" had hit the airwaves recently and was being played regularly on Top 40 radio ("K-I-M-N, Denver 95"). And all the way home—about ten blocks for me—the three of us kept singing, again and again, the signature lines of the song:

"Duke, Duke, Duke, Duke of Earl.
"Duke, Duke, Duke of Earl.
"Duke, Duke, Duke of Earl."

We didn't yet know all the other lyrics, but we knew those lines, and we sang them over and over.

When I recall that episode, I think of it as perhaps the last carefree moment of my life. I had no worries about getting a job, getting into college, war and peace, crime and punishment, or any issue weightier than whether a certain girl who had attracted my earnest attention would find me worth going out with. Just three friends, trying with our changing adolescent voices to hit the low notes of "Duke of Earl."

I didn't realize it then, but carefree was already out of the question for me. I was a black boy from a black family living among white people in a country that was trying to decide whether it would do the right thing—or not. Carefree was not an option.

Three incidents underscored that. The first was one of those things that had absolutely nothing to do with me but, because this was America, had everything to do with me. Sometime during my time at Machebeuf, a young white girl was murdered, allegedly by a black boy, a fellow student of hers at Morey Junior High School in Denver. The story was heavily covered in the newspapers and on television. The coverage included a photo that ran in the Denver Post showing the young suspect, under arrest, being perp-walked to a lockup. The boy was wearing a shirt that was very popular that season: a collared long-sleeve shirt with broad stripes of alternating colors—gold and red or gold and blue.

I had two of those shirts. They were precious to me because I had bought them with my own money—money I earned mowing the lawn of a neighbor, Mr. Bill Bendl, and shoveling the sidewalks of a lady whose house I passed each morning on the way to school, Mrs. McGovern. Indeed, those shirts were the first items of clothing I had ever bought by myself, for myself.

Not long after that picture appeared in the newspaper, I strode into the kitchen one morning, dressed for school in one of those shirts. Mother looked up, saw me, and barked, "Why are you wearing that old ... Morey shirt?"

Emily Wycliff, a child of the Old South, understood the tendency of white folks to lump all black people together as criminals or troublemakers. I'm sure she thought there was no point in making it easier for them to do so than it already was. Or maybe it was that she didn't want to be reminded of an event that had brought shame on the black community. In either case, my treasured "Morey shirt" had suddenly become like a mark of Cain.

The second incident was something of far greater significance for the world—and for me. In October 1962, the Cuban Missile Crisis brought the nation and the world to the brink of nuclear war between the United States and the Soviet Union. The crisis built over several days toward a climax, and I followed it on TV news broadcasts and in the newspaper, growing increasingly apprehensive.

On the day when tensions reached their peak, I just knew that my life and those of all the people I loved were about to end. I skipped basketball practice after classes that day and raced home. Nuclear war was a time to be with family.

I remember burying my face in my dad's lap that evening, crying and wondering aloud why my life had to end before it had really begun. I don't remember what Daddy said to calm and soothe me. Maybe he just let me cry it out. In any case, the Soviets ultimately backed down, and life—mine and humankind's—went on. But there was no carefree living in the shadow of The Bomb.

The last incident involved my one and only attempt before I went to college to ask a girl for a date. She was a skinny girl with auburn hair and a freckled face, probably no prettier than two dozen others in my classes. But for some reason, I took a fancy to her. I couldn't get her out of my mind. I would wake up thinking about her. I lived for the moments during the school day when I would pass her in the halls or see her in class. I imagined myself performing some heroic action that would win her undying passion and affection. And I wondered how, without a car, I could take her out on a date, assuming I could ever work up the courage to ask her out.

In the end, I needn't have wondered or worried. I finally did work up the courage—love will find a way—and I did ask her out. Her response was like that of someone whose cat has just dropped a dead rodent, a trophy of its hunt, on the front doorstep. She could neither formulate a coherent sentence of rejection nor find an exit from the room quickly enough. I was rejected.

* * *

Top 40 rock and roll may have provided the soundtrack of my life in those first two years of high school, but my musical taste began to broaden then, also. In my sophomore year, I had an English teacher named Mr. Reiss. He was a short, dark-haired fellow who wore a mustache—unusual in those days. It was he who introduced me and all my classmates to the singer Joan Baez. This happened while we were studying early English literature. He played a Vanguard recording of Baez singing a medieval song called "Geordie," about a young fellow who "stole sixteen of the king's royal deer" and was sentenced to hang as punishment. He played another tune, "Matty Groves," about a young swain who slept with a nobleman's young wife, was caught in the act and slain as a result. I was captivated by Baez's crystalline voice and by the discovery that "literature" inhabited precincts other than the pages of textbooks. Mr. Reiss flicked on an intellectual switch in my mind.

Mr. Kean taught history and coached the track team. I never took a class from him, but I ran track—slowly—and high-jumped. I'm afraid I was a source of enormous frustration to Mr. Kean. I could clear the high jump bar by a foot with most of my body, but I never learned in those pre-Fosbury flop days to kick my trailing leg. So I'd always bring the bar down with my foot.

In my sophomore year, I made the varsity basketball team, but only as a sub. I mostly rode the bench and watched fellows like Bill Molitor and Tom Wolf and Dan Kellogg and Ed Rumpf play. I distinguished myself in only one way: I could dunk the basketball. I had finally learned how to convert horizontal speed into a vertical leap. I actually could touch the basketball rim with my elbow. But I was uncoordinated otherwise and remained skinny and underweight. So my dunks came only in pre-game warmups. They were good for wowing the crowd, but not much more.

I liked the varsity basketball coach, Fred Howell. He was a former University of Denver player who had migrated to Colorado from Brooklyn. He loved the game, and he loved to talk.

School was the center of my life in those years, but not the entirety of it. Mother and Daddy had become involved in something called the Christian Family Movement, and one of the things that happened as a result of it was a visit to our home one Sunday afternoon by a man from Africa. Mr. Simbananiye was from Burundi. He was the first African I had ever met, and his visit left me eager to learn more about the continent.

I have been lucky enough to visit Africa twice as an adult, but those experiences amounted to nothing more than scratching the surface of all that there is to see and learn about so vast and varied a place. Someday ...

CHAPTER 9

BANKS OF THE WABASH

When my sophomore year of high school ended in spring 1963, I had no reason to think I wouldn't be back at Machebeuf in the fall. I'd probably be a starter on the varsity basketball team. I'd have learned how to kick my trailing leg and become a pretty good high jumper. I'd still be on the student council. And I'd be closer to finding a way to get that girl I liked so much to like me back. Life was good—or was going to be.

Then my world was turned upside down.

In June, Daddy got word that he was being transferred, this time to the federal penitentiary in Terre Haute, Indiana. Unlike the prisons in Ashland and Englewood, the one in Terre Haute was for adults. Daddy wasn't keen on working in adult prisons. And this transfer was a lateral move, without a promotion.

Of course, when Daddy was transferred, we all were transferred. And because it was summertime, there was no chance for me to say goodbye to my school friends, get addresses and phone numbers, and otherwise get my affairs in order. We just left Denver.

The parents had already planned a family trip to Cincinnati to visit Francois, who by then had taken his final vows and was Brother Thaddeus Wycliff. On the way, we stopped in Terre Haute to look the town over. A small discovery: Terre Haute was the home base of Clabber Girl baking powder, which had been part of our household ever since I could remember.

There was one Catholic high school in the city, Paul Schulte High, so Karen and I knew where we would be going in the fall. I don't remember whether it was on that trip or at another time that Mother and Daddy found the house where we would live. It was an old place, a one-story house at 712 N. 15th Street, on the north side of the city. It had that brown, faux-brick asphalt siding and a wide front porch. But like all the houses we lived in, it was too small for our family.

Somehow, as a result of our brief stop at Schulte, word got around that I was a physically towering guy and a monster basketball player. I proved disappointing on both accounts.

As usual, Karen, Chris and I spent most of the summer in Dayton with Grandma and Grandpa. At summer's end, Mother and Daddy and the other kids came down from Denver to pick us up so we could head to our new abode in west central Indiana.

The day we packed up to depart Dayton for Terre Haute was August 28, 1963. That was the date of the great March on Washington for Jobs and Freedom, the date on which Dr. Martin Luther King Jr. delivered his immortal "I Have a Dream Speech."

I don't recall when I made the connection between the Civil Rights Movement and my own life; between sit-ins and our inability to stop on the highways for food at restaurants; between public accommodations and our inability to stay overnight at a motel; between the preaching of Dr. King and my own freedom. But I certainly was aware of it by that date.

Our grandparents' black-and-white television set was on all that day, tuned to the CBS broadcast of the proceedings in Washington. I recall feeling a bit of pride when I saw nuns among the marchers to the Lincoln Memorial.

Dr. King's speech came on as I was helping carry suitcases and other luggage out to our brown Chevy Greenbriar van. So I didn't hear the speech in its entirety that day. I caught bits and pieces as I stopped to watch between trips back and forth to the car. I could sense that this entire proceeding was momentous. Black people weren't on television very much then, so I knew this day was different from anything that had gone before.

Our actual trip to Terre Haute is a blur to me. Compared with many of our other trips as a family, it must have been uneventful.

When I arrived at Schulte High, I was befriended by a classmate named Danny Trueblood, and, in the course of being shown around the school, I met the head football coach, Lou Mihajlovich. Mihajlovich had been a high school football star in South Bend, played collegiate football at Indiana University at Bloomington, and then played briefly in the pros with the Los Angeles Dons of the All-American Football Conference and the Green Bay Packers of the NFL. At Schulte, he followed a legend, Pete Varda, a 1950 Notre Dame graduate who had coached all the school's athletic teams from its founding in 1953 until 1960, when he left for greener pastures at nearby Honey Creek High School.

In the space of a minute, Mihajlovich talked me into going out for the football team. It was a decision I would regret for the next three months. Truth be told, I understood football then in only the most rudimentary way. Most of my teammates had played for several years on grade school teams. Some of them, I later realized, had even been recruited to Schulte because of their football skills. I had as much business playing football with those guys as I'd have had in the president's cabinet. Nevertheless, I went out and tried my best.

The pre-season drills were the worst part. We ran laps and wind-sprints to the point of nearly passing out. Lloyd Robbs, an assistant coach and one of the two black teachers on the Schulte faculty, took what felt to me like a sadistic delight in making us suffer. The role of guys of my minimal ability was basically to serve as dummies for the first team offense to block and the running backs—including star running back Mike Harris, the only other black male in my class—to run over. I remember watching one day as Mike ran the ball during a drill. He put a shoulder into Mike Fuller, a stoutly built linebacker, and knocked him about three feet off the ground and onto his back. I made it a point after that never to be in the way when Mike ran the ball.

Once the season started, things weren't so bad. Practices were shorter and, because the entire school was so invested in the team's success, being a member was kind of exciting. Not so exciting that I wanted to do it again the next year, but kind of exciting.

I had one evening of note that season under the Friday night lights. Our opponent was Honey Creek. They were a terrible team, and our starters piled up a huge lead, allowing Coach Mihajlovich to put some of us scrubs into the game in the last quarter. I was playing defensive back—don't ask me why—and I ended up intercepting *two* passes. After the first, I was tackled immediately in the opponent's end zone, giving us a touchback. After the second, however, I began running the ball back up the field toward our end zone. Then I got confused. I saw a teammate, a chubby-cheeked fellow named Richard Ferrara, peeling back to block for me, and I thought I must be running the wrong way. So I turned around and *did* run the wrong way. Eventually, a shout from the sideline, or maybe from a teammate on the field, let me know that I was going the wrong way, and I reversed course again. Finally, a Honey Creek tackler caught up to me and brought me down. I guess I should have been embarrassed, but I was too confused to be embarrassed. At least I didn't cost us the game.

Schulte was a very good school, and my going there turned out to be a stroke of life-changing good fortune. But it took me a long time to appreciate the school because my heart remained in Denver, at Machebeuf, and with that girl that I had been so in love with. And just when I was beginning to get over all that, the scab was ripped off: I learned, through a letter to my sister Karen from one of her friends, about a car crash that had killed my friend Bob Hickey and left another boy permanently paralyzed. Several members of the Machebeuf basketball team had been out joyriding one evening, and the driver lost control of the car and crashed it. Amid my sorrow, it never occurred to me that, had I still been there, I might well have been involved in that accident.

Academically, my transition to Schulte was largely seamless. With the exception of one course, I was enrolled in the same kind of college prep curriculum I had been taking at Machebeuf. I took Latin, English, French, American History, a science course, and religion. My one departure from the college prep track was in math. I took advantage of the move and my parents' momentary inattention to slack off. Instead of taking a second year of algebra, I took a gut course: Business Arithmetic. It was shamefully easy, and I knew in my heart of hearts that I ought to be doing something more demanding, but I didn't.

Before senior year, someone had a talk with me and told me I needed to take a serious math course, so I enrolled in Algebra 2. It was taught by a nun, Sister Joseph Andre. Like all the nuns at Schulte, she was a member of the Sisters of Providence, whose motherhouse, or headquarters, was at St. Mary of the Woods College in nearby West Terre Haute.

While I cannot honestly say that Sister Joseph Andre helped me understand math—I think I already was beyond that possibility by then—she became another of my angels, those people who show up unexpectedly in your life and make good things happen.

I got a C in her course for the first semester, but toward the end of the second semester, I was struggling. I probably was headed for a D in the course, and that could have negated my chances of college acceptance. Sister Joseph Andre took me aside and offered me a deal: If

BEFORE THE BYLINE DON WYCLIFF

I would go during the summer and take an algebra course at Indiana State University in Terre Haute, she would give me a C for the course. I readily agreed and kept the bargain, although I'm not sure I understood algebra any better after that ISU course than before.

Years later, after I had become editorial page editor at the Chicago Tribune, I got a call one day from the security desk in the lobby. The guard said that there was a "Sister Margaret Sullivan" who wanted to see me. I had no idea who Sister Margaret Sullivan was. Then she gave the guard another name, Sister Joseph Andre. I recognized it immediately. Like many nuns after Vatican II, Sister Joseph Andre had resumed her original name, Margaret Sullivan.

She was a member of a well-known and highly regarded Irish Catholic family in Chicago, and she regularly came back to the city from Terre Haute during the summer to visit. After that first visit to the Tribune, she made it a habit to stop by whenever she was in town, and I always looked forward to her visits.

I once asked her why she gave me that break on my algebra grade. She replied, "I liked your family. You were a good Catholic family." It had nothing to do with the Pythagorean theorem, but I'll take that.

Years later, after Sister Margaret had retired and I had moved on to work, briefly, in the administration at Notre Dame, I drove down to Terre Haute to visit her at the motherhouse of the Sisters of Providence. She was proud to introduce her former student to her fellow sisters and have me dine with her and others in the refectory. Seeing her pride in my achievements was more satisfying than any prize I ever won.

Sister Joseph Andre was just one of the teachers at Schulte who had an influence on my life. Avon Gillespie, a music and fine arts teacher and the other of Schulte's two black faculty members, was another. I never took a course with Mr. Gillespie, but I got to know him through "Broadway Omnibus," a year-end production that he managed in which students performed scenes from popular Broadway musicals of the time. I tried out and won a part as a sailor in "South Pacific."

Mr. Gillespie was a devout Catholic, and I recall that at one point he introduced me to a visiting priest, Father Boniface Luykx, a member of a Belgian order called the Premonstratensians. Father Luykx tried mightily to persuade me to join his order and become a missionary to what then was known as the Belgian Congo. I was gracious with him, but he might just as well have been talking to a brick wall: I liked girls—or at least the idea of girls (I hadn't experienced the sexual reality yet)—too much to become a priest and endure a life of celibacy.

After I left Terre Haute, I lost track of him. Then I began hearing from time to time about a liturgical music expert named Avon Gillespie who incorporated African-American musical themes and motifs into Catholic liturgies. I knew it must be Mr. Gillespie from Schulte.

In 2010, shortly before the Schulte Class of 1965 had a reunion in Terre Haute, I went searching for Mr. Gillespie on the internet. I knew that he had taught for a period of time at North Texas State University in Denton. I finally managed to track down a former student of his, who told me that Avon Gillespie had died of AIDS back in 1989. He was only 51 years old. I also learned that he had a daughter, with whom I struck up a brief correspondence.

Another Schulte teacher who influenced me did it almost inadvertently and in a one-way conversation that lasted no more than thirty seconds.

John Seifert, an English teacher, was what passed in those innocent days for an eccentric. He was of middling height and had a head full of wild, reddish hair that he wore just a tad longer than was standard in that era. He often came off in class as gruff and a bit distracted. In fact, I think, he was just absorbed in the language and literature that he was trying to get us to appreciate.

I took Mr. Seifert's English literature course in my senior year. He was the first teacher I ever heard speak in Old English. It was just a few lines, a tiny sample, but it gave me an idea of what that predecessor to modern English must have sounded like. That was good teaching.

It was almost the end of our senior year. We were all looking forward to graduation and getting out of high school. We were feeling our oats. We were, in our minds, grownups. We were also, sometimes, smart alecks.

Mr. Seifert was a no-nonsense kind of guy, and one day, in an effort to discipline one of the senior boys, he and the boy became involved in a physical altercation. This was unheard of at Schulte, and it created a stir among the seniors. Ultimately, the confrontation was defused. I'm not sure how the student was punished—there was no question that he would be. But shortly after the incident, I happened to be walking down an otherwise deserted hallway and saw Mr. Seifert approaching from the other direction. As we met, he stopped and looked at me as if he felt I, at least, would be able to appreciate his words. Then, smiling wryly, he recited the last lines of Matthew Arnold's "Dover Beach," which we had studied just a few days earlier in his class:

> *"And we are here as on a darkling plain*
> *Swept with confused alarms of struggle and flight,*
> *Where ignorant armies clash by night."*

That moment was an epiphany for me. It was the first time I truly appreciated that poetry—all literature, actually—was not just an academic exercise engaged in to get a grade, but was about real human feelings, emotions, actions. It was about real life. It expressed profound truths and insights about human life—and the human condition.

In that brief encounter, John Seifert opened up intellectual life to me.

I told him this one day, many years later. He didn't remember the incident.

At Schulte, as at Machebeuf, I played basketball. Indiana high school basketball was at least one, and probably several cuts in quality above that in the Denver parochial league. Largely due to my jumping ability, I made the team at Schulte. I weighed, at most, 165 pounds in those days. I was tall but not strong enough to be as good a rebounder as my jumping ability should have made me; I could be boxed out too easily by more muscular guys. I was never a great ballhandler, but I was a good defender and, if I may say so, a great shot blocker.

I got to demonstrate this in a game junior year against Wiley High School. Wiley had two outstanding players, both of them black. Creed Hubbard was a Carmelo Anthony-type forward who stood about six foot four or five and moved easily with the ball or without it. Ted Sweatt was a six-foot-seven-inch center, four inches taller than I. He was skinny like me, but a lot better coordinated and more skillful as a ball handler.

We played Wiley in the Indiana State University arena, a new facility at the time. I wasn't a starter, but I did get into the game as a backup center. I served notice of my presence that night when I blocked two of Sweatt's shots. The second one I can still see in my mind's eye. He skyed above the rim, and I did the same, managing to flick the ball away just as he was about to release it.

Ted Sweatt later became the only person I knew personally who was killed in Vietnam.

In my senior year, my best game was against State High School, the lab school for Indiana State University. I blocked fifteen shots that night. I wasn't terribly disciplined—I ranged all over the court, swatting away balls thrown up by all of their players. The next day, one of my teachers expressed wonderment at my performance, probably the only time anybody ever did that in a complimentary way.

In Indiana in those days, the regular basketball season was like a warmup for the state tournament. Every team played in the tourna-

BEFORE THE BYLINE DON WYCLIFF

ment, no matter how well or badly it had done during the regular season. There were no class groupings. Every school, big or small, urban or rural, was in the running for the one state crown. In junior year, with a team of three seniors and twelve juniors, we compiled a regular-season record of only three wins and fifteen losses. Nevertheless, when the sectional round of the state tourney arrived, we were ready. We knocked off two favored teams in our first two games and made it to the sectional finals, where we played Garfield High School, whose star was Frank Hamblen, later an assistant coach of the Chicago Bulls and the Los Angeles Lakers under the great Phil Jackson. We ended up losing the sectional championship game in overtime.

In my senior year, we had a terrific team—almost all seniors—and compiled a season record of fifteen wins and three losses. We were favored to win the sectionals. But we ended up losing in the first round to State High School, whom we had beaten badly during the season.

Our head basketball coach was Mark LaGrange, who was also a mathematics teacher. He was a nice man—too nice, I thought. I was used to the fiery Brooklynite, Fred Howell, who had been my coach in Denver. LaGrange smiled constantly. He never raised his voice or shouted at a referee. He seemed phlegmatic. He seemed never to speak more than two sentences without using the phrase "from the standpoint that."

I liked LaGrange, but one incident left me permanently annoyed with him. It was Friday, November 22, 1963, and it was a free day at Schulte—one of those teacher training days or something. There were no classes, but we did have a basketball practice scheduled around midday. Shortly after I had dressed for practice and gotten out onto the basketball court, Father Joseph Beechem, the principal, turned on the public address system and began piping over it radio reports of the shooting, and then the death, of President John F. Kennedy in Dallas. I thought Coach LaGrange would surely call off practice and send us home. He didn't. We continued to practice for about two hours. I, at least, was unable to focus, thinking about the assassination, a world-shattering event. Finally, we were released to go home, to spend the next four days like virtually everyone else in the nation: huddled with family in front of our television sets, watching the aftermath of the assassination, including the murder on live TV of the assassin, Lee Harvey Oswald, and the solemnity of the presidential funeral.

At Schulte, as at Machebeuf, I had no life beyond school and home. If I wasn't at school in class or in some extracurricular activity, I was at home. Like everybody else in the household, I had my chores. The most important of them was to maintain the furnace, clearing out spent coal and putting in fresh. I used to pride myself on being able to remove the spent coal in a perfect circle of glowing embers.

But my main chore, and that of all my brothers and sisters, was to study, to do well in school, to be a credit to ourselves, our family, our race. Daddy and Mother had drilled that sense of obligation into us, and I was on automatic pilot in that regard. The house may have been crowded, but we all were diligent students, so it wasn't a matter of rowing against the tide.

In my junior year, Karen and I used to ride to Schulte with a senior girl, Connie Burns, and her younger brother Fred. I'll never forget the sense of excitement that pervaded the car on the Monday morning in February 1964 after the Beatles appeared for the first time on the Ed Sullivan Show. It was as if we all had witnessed something that could be seen only by people with young eyes, and we shared a delicious open secret.

Like my dad in his time, I enjoyed some success as a student politician. With the help of a contingent of committed supporters, including our class valedictorian Penny Higgins, I won election as Schulte's student body president. That provided me with my initiation into presidential politics in the autumn of my senior year. The contest that year,

BEFORE THE BYLINE DON WYCLIFF

1964, was between the Democratic incumbent, Lyndon Johnson, and the Republican challenger, Barry Goldwater. For some reason, William Miller, the congressman from Buffalo who was Goldwater's vice presidential running mate, decided during a trip to Terre Haute to visit Schulte.

It was my duty as student body president to introduce Miller at an outdoor assembly. After Miller's speech, an aide approached me and asked whether I would lead the audience in the pledge of allegiance at a rally that night at the ISU arena downtown. I said I'd have to ask my parents. I went home and asked Mother's permission, which she granted. So I made my way downtown that night and led the pledge. And then I became a Goldwater supporter.

There was, in those days, something appealing to me about people who spoke with an air of certainty about whatever they were talking about. Goldwater seemed to do that. Fortunately, nobody paid attention to me back then. Johnson won by a landslide. I grew in age and wisdom and grace—and became a Democrat. But in my first foray into presidential politics, I managed to be on the wrong side of the election, and of history.

There was another notable part of that fall of 1964: Under new coach Ara Parseghian, the University of Notre Dame came within minutes of an unbeaten football season and a national championship.

I used to listen to the Notre Dame games in the garage behind our house, on the radio of a decrepit little Renault sedan. The car had belonged to a son of Berneatha Mosley Bullock, one of Daddy's childhood friends. Daddy had co-signed the car loan for him, and somehow the car eventually became ours.

You'd have thought I had money on those games, so emotionally invested was I in Notre Dame's success. I knew Notre Dame was in South Bend, Indiana, because the announcers kept saying that, but I had no sense of where that was in relation to Terre Haute. And I certainly never entertained the notion of going to school there. As far as I was concerned, Notre Dame, like Hollywood, existed in some ethereal realm inhabited by people utterly unlike me.

Even though I was taking a college prep curriculum at Schulte, I hadn't given much thought to what college I might attend when the time came. Part of the problem was that college itself was mysterious to me. What was a credit hour? Did everybody have to be in a fraternity? Did people really spend their time stuffing themselves into phone booths and swallowing goldfish, as I had seen in Look and Life magazines? And what about those college students I had read about who went down South to work for civil rights—how did they manage that?

Daddy had gone to college at Texas Southern University, but I never talked with him about it. Francois was going to college—the Brothers of the Poor of St. Francis were sending him to Xavier University in Cincinnati—but he was in a monastery and unavailable to talk to about it. Indiana State University was right in downtown Terre Haute, no more than a mile or two from our house, but I had no idea how to even approach the place. There probably was a counselor at Schulte who could have helped me figure things out, but I didn't know who it was.

Early in 1965, in my last semester of high school, I sent away for applications and information about the two schools with which my family had connections, Xavier and Texas Southern. About the same time, I began visiting the offices of the local military recruiters. The Marines particularly appealed to me because they were said to be the toughest of the services and "builders of men." I imagined that they could turn my skinny, 165-pound body into something I would feel good looking at in the mirror in the morning. The Marine Corps recruiter was Sergeant Harvey Gunnels. He looked to be about five foot ten, and he impressed the hell out of me.

Also, early in 1965, Grandpa fell ill. Grandpa had always been a rock. He used to come back from his rare visits to the doctor and say the doctor had described him as a "pine knot," hard and tough. He had taken care of Grandma since she fell ill with bad diabetes back in the mid-1950s. The idea that Grandpa was seriously ill—it turned out to be stomach cancer, and fatal—just didn't compute for me.

Because of Grandpa's illness, Daddy was away from us for a considerable time during the winter and spring of that year, seeing after Grandpa and Grandma in Dayton. During one of those absences, I finally mustered the courage to ask Mother for the money I needed to apply to Xavier.

I'll never forget that day. She was mopping the kitchen floor. I walked up behind her and said, "Mother, can I have $15?" I remember how she whirled around and, with a look almost of terror on her face, asked me, "For what?" I told her it was the application fee for Xavier. She said she would have to think about it.

I assume she later talked about it by phone with Daddy, and they agreed to give me the money. So I sent off the only college application I planned to submit.

A few weeks later, the word came back from Xavier. I had won admission and a full-tuition scholarship. I was excited, but worried. Suddenly, college seemed within my reach—but still out of reach. Room and board could not be cheap, and I had no idea how I would raise the money for that.

I told Father Beechem about my admission to Xavier and the scholarship. Unknown to me, he was on the lookout for additional help for me and, I suspect, for others at Schulte. One day, he called me in and told me about a scholarship being offered for the first time that year by the Archdiocese of Indianapolis for a black student at one of its high schools. Like the Xavier scholarship I had already received, the archdiocesan scholarship was to be used for tuition, not other expenses. Nevertheless, Father Beechem urged me to apply. And when word came that I was invited to Indianapolis for an interview with the scholarship selection committee, he insisted I go.

There were three interviewers on the committee, and they told me that, had I not already had the Xavier scholarship, I would have been their choice for the archdiocese's award. I went home thinking that was the end of my business with those people.

Then a few days later, the phone rang. Mother took the call in the kitchen and talked politely with someone for several minutes. Then she came out to the living room and asked me, "Do you know a Mr. Patrick Fisher?"

"Yes," I replied. "He was one of the people who interviewed me in Indianapolis the other day."

"Well," Mother said, "he wanted to know whether you would be interested in going to the University of Notre Dame."

If I had known then what I know now, my response would have been along the lines of "Is the Pope Catholic?" But in those days, I had no full appreciation of the Notre Dame mystique and the school's mythic significance among American Catholics and in American life generally.

Most of what I did know was related to their sports programs: I knew it had a famous football team; I knew it had once had a football coach named Frank Leahy, because one of his children, a big, redheaded lad named Jim Leahy, had been a classmate and a friend of mine at Machebeuf in Denver; and I knew that Notre Dame had once had a standout basketball player—a fellow named Tom Hawkins—who was, like me, a "Negro" in the terminology of that time. Hawkins became an all-American at Notre Dame and went on to play professional basketball with the Lakers, first in Minneapolis and later in Los Angeles. I recalled reading a story about him sometime during the 1950s in Boys' Life magazine, and his name stuck in my mind.

Patrick Fisher was a member of the undergraduate class of 1935 at Notre Dame and a 1937 graduate of the university's law school. He practiced law in Indianapolis and was a dedicated layman in the archdiocese.

After that phone conversation with Mother, everything happened rapidly. On a Sunday not long afterwards, while our family was driving from Terre Haute to Cincinnati to visit Francois, we stopped at Mr. Fisher's law office in Indianapolis. I filled out the application for admission to Notre Dame while he and my parents talked. When I finished, Daddy opened his wallet and handed Mr. Fisher the application fee—I think it was $15—in cash. And then we left for Cincinnati to visit Francois—Brother Thaddeus—at Mt. Alverno, the motherhouse of the Brothers of the Poor of St. Francis.

A short time later, word came that I had been admitted to Notre Dame and given a scholarship to cover all expenses—tuition, room and board. The scholarship's donor was anonymous to me and remains so to this day.

In the space of a month, my confusion about my post-graduation future had been dispelled, and a completely unexpected future opened for me. And not just for me but, as it turned out, for our whole family.

CHAPTER 10
TO DU LAC

I graduated from Schulte on Sunday, June 6, 1965. The next morning, along with Mother and my seven younger siblings, I piled into the Chevy Greenbriar van and began driving south to Texas. Daddy was already there. He had gone down a couple of weeks earlier after Grandpa took a turn for the worse.

On Sunday, June 13, Grandpa died. He passed away in his own bed in his own house. He had withered to little more than a stick figure, and in his last days was so weak it wasn't really possible to hold a conversation with him. He had a hole in his abdomen, and a tube and a colostomy bag dangled from it. I stood at the foot of the bed that Sunday morning and watched as he breathed faster and faster and faster, and then, with his mouth and his eyes wide open, stopped breathing and went silent. A short time later, Dr. Ernest Richter came and pronounced him dead.

I cried mightily that morning. Grandpa meant the world to me. I wanted nothing more than for him to be proud of me. I had never gotten to tell him that I would be going to one of the most famous colleges in the country.

He was buried in the cemetery in Ames. His funeral was one of the biggest I have ever been to, with hundreds of people in attendance.

BEFORE THE BYLINE DON WYCLIFF

With Grandpa gone, the shop was closed, and there was no work for me in Dayton. So I returned to Terre Haute after his funeral. That summer would be the first in my life that I did not spend in Dayton, Texas. I enrolled in that algebra course at Indiana State that I had promised Sister Joseph Andre I would take. And I began looking for a summer job.

I found one working as a helper on a delivery truck for a furniture store. The pay was $1.25 per hour, which I considered quite good. But I soon had to quit when I was unable to resolve a schedule conflict between the job and my math course. The next couple of weeks were among the longest and most miserable of my young life. I had no money, no job and no prospect of either. Then a neighbor, Mrs. Helen Terstegge, who had two kids at Schulte and who worked as a waitress in the restaurant at the Albert Pick Motel just outside Terre Haute, told Mother about an opening for a dishwasher at the restaurant.

I promptly made my way out there, applied for the job and was hired by the manager, a short, fat, foppish man named Andre Gavion. The pay was 85 cents an hour. Besides washing dishes, I was responsible for busing tables and delivering room-service orders to guests at the motel. I was glad to do it all, as long as I had a job.

I drove to work each day in that old Renault sedan. The engine was in such bad shape that the car couldn't go faster than forty miles per hour. I had to rev the engine for a good ten seconds or so before I could ease my foot off the clutch and slowly pull away from wherever it was stopped, trailed by a cloud of dark exhaust. As a result, I learned to time my approaches to traffic lights to avoid having to stop. But at least the Renault moved and would get me the few miles from our house to the Albert Pick, and back.

Whatever its other shortcomings, the car had a functioning radio, and that was crucial in the summer of 1965. For that was the summer of Sonny and Cher and "I Got You, Babe," of the Righteous Brothers'

"You've Lost That Loving Feeling," of a whole raft of Motown hits by Mary Wells, Marvin Gaye and others, of Bob Dylan's "Like a Rolling Stone," of Barry McGuire with "The Eve of Destruction."

The kitchen crew at the Albert Pick were an amusing lot. A Hollywood producer could have made a sitcom out of them. There was Evie, the salad lady—short, fiftyish, blonde, slightly airheaded and lovable. There was Archie, the cook—tall, light-skinned, African-American (the only one in the crew besides me), brash and assertive ("If I don't work, nobody works!"). There was Jim, the dishwasher on the shift before my late-afternoon shift—short, blond, thick glasses, awfully nice but not real bright. I recall how, at the end of the summer, when it was time for me to depart for Notre Dame, Jim, who was in his early 20s, and I had a conversation during which he allowed that he was thinking he might try college ... someday ... perhaps ... maybe ...

And at the end of the summer, there was Dave, a high schooler who came on a couple of weeks before my departure. I was supposed to train him to replace me. I don't remember much about Dave except that, when I saw the way he washed dishes, I was glad I never went to the Albert Pick as a customer.

From childhood, I had absorbed a litany of lessons from Emily Wycliff, and I always worked with them playing in my head like a recording on an endless loop: "Don't *half-do* your work." "Do it the way you would do it if you had to eat off those plates." So I would use the spray nozzle to get the bulk of the food off before stacking the dishes into the rack. I'd inspect them as they came out of the washer to make sure there was no food still caked on them. Not so, Dave. They paid him minimum wage, and he gave them minimal work.

I learned a lot that summer about relating to people in the workplace, and I had some interesting experiences. Among them: Delivering room service to the reigning Miss Indiana, whom I found in bed with a boyfriend. She had her little Corvair convertible parked outside her room, with her first name stenciled on the driver's side door.

Eventually, mid-September arrived, and it was time for me to go to college. My departure coincided with the departure of the rest of the family from Terre Haute for Ashland. Daddy was being transferred again after only two years, and again without a promotion. This was becoming a cause of increasing anger for Mother, who discerned racism in it. Daddy did not say what he thought about it, at least not in my presence. But it got worse. The family was in Ashland only one year before Daddy was transferred again, this time to the National Training Center, a youth institution, in Washington, D.C. And two years after that, he was sent to the Federal Correctional Institution in Texarkana, Texas. So while I entered college from Terre Haute, I finished as a resident of Texarkana, and had two other homes in between. There was one consolation in the Texarkana move: The family lived on "the reservation," a compound next to the prison reserved for high-level employees. The Wycliffs were the first black family to do that in Texarkana.

Mother and the other children went to Ashland by train. The morning of Friday, September 17, 1965, Daddy and I got up, packed my things into the Greenbriar and set out for Notre Dame. It was a sunny, warm, late-summer day. We got there in time for the start of freshman orientation that afternoon.

I checked into my dorm, Farley Hall; met the rector, Father James Buckley, and got the key to my room, Number 237. The presence of bunk beds in the room told me it was a double. I was the first to arrive. I claimed the lower bunk.

Later in the afternoon, my roommate showed up with his dad. A momentary flash of surprise crossed his face, but Steve Foss never betrayed any discomfort with having a black roommate. We got along well and even roomed together again in junior year, after he returned from his sophomore year abroad in Innsbruck, Austria.

Steve was from Albuquerque, New Mexico. He was a musician—a

drummer—and a German language major. His father was a professor at a small Catholic college in Albuquerque; I can't remember his field. Steve was slender, blond, and about five feet ten inches tall. And he was the most religiously irreverent person I had met to that point in my sheltered Catholic life.

On our second Sunday at Notre Dame, Steve decided he was not going to Mass. So concerned was I to "save his soul" that I literally dragged him out of his top bunk and made him come with me to Mass in the Farley Hall chapel. But that didn't continue. I soon realized that I couldn't save Foss's soul for him, and he didn't want to save it, so I let him sleep.

Residence hall life was then and remains now of the essence of a Notre Dame education. There are no fraternities, so the residence hall is the center of most students' non-classroom life. Until 1965, however, freshmen were segregated in halls occupied solely by freshmen, which could produce conditions resembling those in a bad fraternity house. In fall 1965, Farley became one of the first "stay halls," housing students from all four classes. Those of us who lived there were involved in something of an experiment.

It's funny how things develop in neighborhoods. You can have neighbors on all sides of you, and you become friends with some and are barely on nodding terms with others. That's what happened to Foss and me. In a triple on one side of us were freshmen David White from Arlington, Massachusetts; Jeff Davis from Fullerton, California, and Joel Connelly from Bellingham, Washington. The five of us became pretty friendly, spending nearly as much time in each other's rooms as in our own. The guys who lived on the other side of us, I can't even remember. Directly across the hall from my and Foss's room was a little closet with a single pay phone in it. That's where everybody on the floor came to make or receive calls in those days before Notre Dame installed telephones in each dorm room. Next door to the phone room was the shower and toilet facility, a big room with about half a dozen shower stalls, an equal number of toilets and some urinals.

Just past White-Davis-Connelly's room on an intersecting corridor was that of Bob Whitmore and Dwight Murphy, freshmen who were scholarship basketball players and two of the nine black students in the 1,600-man entering class of 1965. Bob and Dwight used to play ferocious games of cards when they weren't practicing, in class or studying. Bob was about six foot seven; Dwight was about six foot five. After watching them practice, I abandoned any ambitions I had of trying to win a spot on the freshman team as a walk-on.

Next door to Bob and Dwight was another triple, this one occupied by a sophomore named Michael Lehan and two roommates. Lehan, short, dark-haired, smart and funny, became one of my best friends. I visited his home in tiny Dunlap, Iowa. I got to know his parents. Mike and I worked together two summers as counselors in the Notre Dame Upward Bound program. And we did some traveling together when Mike was a senior and I was a junior.

Daddy stayed in South Bend that Friday night of orientation weekend and attended some events for parents. Then, on Saturday afternoon, he bid me goodbye and drove away. I had been eager to get to Notre Dame and begin the next chapter of my life, but it wasn't until that moment of parting that I realized how much I was going to miss my family. I was now on my own. I was still *of* my family, but I was no longer *in* it. And that was scary.

The fear didn't last long. On Monday morning, classes started, and the daily routines of college life began to transform strangers into friends and friends into a community. Life revolved around classes, of course, and most of us had at least five. I also had a scholarship that required a 3.0 grade point average. So I ran scared from day one.

I entered Notre Dame intending to major in political science. First, John F. Kennedy, and then the Civil Rights Movement, had convinced me of the transcendent importance of politics. Kennedy's rhetoric suggested all the noble things that could be achieved through politics; the Civil Rights Movement demonstrated the real improvements that politics could create. I wanted to learn about it in depth.

My schedule that first semester included one government course, Political Order, taught by a young assistant professor named Walter Nicgorski. But instead of lecturing about parties and elections and polls, Nicgorski talked about concepts like ethics and justice and citizenship. Instead of popular works about current political issues, he had us read parts of Thucydides' "The Peloponessian War," and Aristotle's "Nicomachean Ethics," along with selections from "The Federalist."

At first, I was confused: What did these books and concepts have to do with politics, with who won elections and what bills got passed by Congress? Over time, however, I began to discern the connections, to realize what a superficial understanding of politics I had had, and to appreciate the vastly more profound understanding that Professor Nicgorski was leading me to. I began to understand how much I didn't know, and that, Plato said, is the beginning of all learning.

I ended up getting an A from Professor Nicgorski that first semester. But I got more than a good grade. I got a mentor. He took me under his wing, guided me, wrote letters of recommendation for me, and hired me as his research assistant.

I experienced a similar epiphany in my theology class. In those days, Notre Dame was far more prescriptive in its curriculum than it is now. We were required to take one course in philosophy and one in theology each year. My theology course was on scripture and was taught by a fellow named John Halligan. My puerile, Catholic school understanding of scripture began to be replaced by one far more sophisticated and subtle. I was learning to think critically.

Notre Dame was still an all-male school in 1965—it wouldn't begin admitting women as undergraduates until 1972. And in many respects, it had more in common with monasteries than with most other universities. Those attributes, combined with its relative isolation in South Bend, Indiana, made for lonely times most of the academic year.

But on fall football weekends, the monastery turned into a veritable carnival, as visitors from all over the country—and occasionally a national television network—converged on the campus to watch the Fighting Irish play.

Each of the dorms would set up a stand to sell hot dogs, burgers or other foods. Bands would play on the quads. And girls would descend on the campus.

It was customary on Saturday evenings after home football games for the student union to sponsor on-campus concerts by big-name performers. During my time on campus, we had such acts as the Supremes, Motown's biggest stars at the time, the Righteous Brothers, the Fifth Dimension, and Dionne Warwick.

But two acts during my freshman year stood out, for different reasons. One of the year's first concerts was by Little Anthony and the Imperials, a doo-wop group that had had several big hits in the late 1950s, gone into eclipse, and then made a comeback in the mid-1960s. They were favorites of mine. I've always been a sucker for romantic ballads like their "Goin' Out of My Head," "Hurt So Bad," and "On the Outside Looking In."

I went to the concert at Stepan Center and somehow ended up very close to the stage—close enough that I could see the beads of perspiration on the group members' faces as they performed. And I suddenly found myself having the same feeling I had had years earlier when Daddy took us all to see the Milwaukee Braves play the Cincinnati Redlegs at Crosley Field in Cincinnati. I couldn't believe I was in the same room, breathing the same air as these big-name performers who previously had existed for me only as voices issuing from behind an AM radio dial. Surely this place, this University of Notre Dame, must be over the rainbow.

My amazement and gratitude grew even deeper later as I realized what a gift I had been given: Here I was, enjoying all of this—an education, housing, food—for free.

The other memorable concert was by the folksinging group the Kingston Trio. This concert was special because it was my first date.

On a Friday evening in November, I was in the dinner line at the North Dining Hall when a fellow I didn't know walked up and introduced himself. He was Lou Pignatelli, the sophomore class president. He explained that a friend of his, the president of the student body at Roosevelt University in Chicago, was coming to campus the next day for the football game and the concert to follow. His friend was black, and Pignatelli was trying to line up a date for him at St. Mary's College. He had found a young black woman who would go with him to the concert, but she wanted him to find a date for her roommate as well. Would I be interested in a blind date?

Adopting my best devil-may-care pose—I didn't want to let on that I had never had a date before—I said yes, I would do it. And so it was arranged.

In those days, it was customary to dress up to go to a concert. That meant suit, tie and well-shined shoes. I went back to my dorm and pulled out my one suit. It had been a high school graduation gift from my parents. Tall, skinny, and gangly, I had always had trouble buying clothes off the rack. So Mother and Daddy had a suit tailor-made for me by probably the only black tailor in Terre Haute. I remember the day we picked it up. I put that suit on and it fit perfectly. What a wonderful feeling!

However, by the time I was ready to use it for the first time, I had put on at least 15 pounds, going from 165 when I arrived on campus to 180 or so in November. So when I went to put my suit on that Saturday evening, I discovered that it was no longer a perfect fit. It was almost a no-fit.

BEFORE THE BYLINE DON WYCLIFF

I managed to suck my gut in enough to fasten the trousers and zip the fly, and I cinched my belt tightly enough that I could keep things together as long as I didn't make any false moves.

The guy from Roosevelt and I walked over to St. Mary's to pick up our dates. When the two young women walked into the lounge at their dorm, it was clear right away that there was a physical mismatch. The other fellow was about five foot eight and was matched up with Maria Nickens, a young lady from Washington, D.C., who was about five foot five. I, at six foot three, was matched with her roommate, a young woman from New Orleans named Mabel ("Embie") Benjamin, who couldn't have been more than five feet tall.

We made our way back to the Notre Dame campus and to Stepan Center, a geodesic dome at the north end of campus where concerts were held in those days. We enjoyed the concert. And then it was time to get the ladies back to St. Mary's.

Both St. Mary's and Notre Dame had curfews in those days, and they were earlier for freshmen than for upperclassmen and women. We realized that if we didn't put a whip to our horses, Maria and Embie were going to be late. So we decided to take a taxi instead of walking back to SMC. We hurried to the traffic circle at the front of campus, where taxis lined up. All this time, I was holding my breath and suffering with my too-tight suit pants.

At the circle, we stood on the curb waiting for a taxi to pull up. When I saw one approaching. I stepped off the curb to hail it, as I thought I had seen done in movies and on television. The cab came toward us, and I stepped backward, up onto the curb. I also stepped into a wire that had been strung at about knee level to keep people off the grass. I tumbled backwards onto the grass, landing on my back. I wasn't hurt physically, but my delicate pride took a grievous hit as my pants split.

Oh, the embarrassment! I never got over it. Even though I liked both Maria and Embie, I never could muster the courage to ask either of them out again. That probably was profoundly foolish, but that's the way I was in those days. Such vanity!

Later in that freshman year, I attended a house party off campus with some of the other black students. There, I met a beautiful, brown-skinned young woman who introduced herself as Sylvia Scott. I was immediately, deeply smitten. It turned out that Sylvia went more commonly by her middle name, Kay. We started dating. I took her to her junior prom at South Bend Central High School. I met her parents, Ginny and Jimmy, and her sister, Toni. They became like a family away from home for me. And even after Kay and I no longer dated, I remained attached to her family. Truthfully, had it not been for the Scott family, I might not have survived that first year at Notre Dame.

Very early in my freshman year, I joined CONE, the Committee on Negro Enrollment, a student government effort to increase the paltry number of black students at Notre Dame. In my class, there were only nine black students, and we doubled the number in the university as a whole.

CONE had been created by Algernon "Jay" Cooper, a black upperclassman from Mobile, Alabama. After graduating from Notre Dame in 1966, Jay went on to become a lawyer and a politician in his home state. When I joined CONE, it was being run by Stephen Weeg, a white sophomore from Rockford, Illinois, who went on to become a leading liberal figure in politics in Idaho.

One of Notre Dame's most distinguished black graduates, former Air Force General Francis X. Taylor, credits a talk I gave at Washington's Dunbar High School with inspiring him to apply to Notre Dame. Honestly, I don't remember that talk or a trip to Washington during my freshman year. But I do recall two other CONE-related trips. One, taken during a break from classes sometime during the winter months, was to Charleston, West Virginia. I took a bus from Ashland to Charles-

BEFORE THE BYLINE DON WYCLIFF

ton to speak at a school there. I remember the West Virginia landscape, mountainous and rolling. I liked it.

The other trip was during my junior year, when I served as chairman of CONE. A white classmate, Eric Weischaus, had joined the group, and Eric was very ardent about our cause. One day in the spring semester of 1968, we went together to talk to the Notre Dame alumni club in Chicago, a natural recruiting ground for the university.

The guy running the program that evening was a West Side politician, and his every word and action communicated to me that he viewed us—Eric and me and our cause—as at best a distraction from the main business of the evening, which was to socialize. So did the behavior of the rest of those in attendance.

The time came for Eric and me to speak. I went first and talked about the need to increase black enrollment, about the opportunity Chicago offered, and how we needed alumni help to take advantage of that opportunity. I spoke for about five minutes. Then Eric got up to talk. He was passionate. He also, it soon became clear, was being ignored. There were side conversations going on in the audience. Still, Eric kept trying. Finally, I leaned over and pulled his coat and whispered that they weren't paying attention. So he wrapped up, and the emcee gave us the bum's rush off the stage.

I've wondered from time to time whether those Chicago alumni would have paid closer attention that evening if they had known that the white fellow they were ignoring would become, twenty-five years later, Notre Dame's first and, so far, only Nobel laureate. Eric Weischaus became a professor at Princeton and won the Nobel Prize in 1995 for biochemistry.

My other main activity early on was the ROTC drill team. Notre Dame required freshmen to take a one-credit course in either ROTC or physical education. To pass the physical education course, you had to learn to swim. I was terrified of deep water and the swimming requirement, so I chose Army ROTC, where I remained enrolled through my sophomore year.

I joined the drill team, but it turned out that I wasn't very handy at twirling rifles. So they made me the guidon bearer. That was a bit of a disappointment. Nevertheless, thanks to the drill team, I got to travel around the Midwest—to Peoria, Madison, St. Louis, and Detroit.

My world was expanding, and Notre Dame was the reason.

BEFORE THE BYLINE DON WYCLIFF

CHAPTER 11
BEST OF TIMES

If I could relive any part of my early life, it would be my last two years of college, from the summer of 1967 to the summer of 1969. The world seemed then to be flying apart, what with the Vietnam War and the protests it inspired; the Soviet invasion of Czechoslovakia and suppression of the Prague Spring; the assassinations of Dr. Martin Luther King Jr. and Senator Robert F. Kennedy; the pitched battles between Chicago police and protestors at the 1968 Democratic National Convention; and the black rebellions in Newark, Detroit, Milwaukee and other cities.

But for me at Notre Dame, everything seemed finally to be coming together. By the start of my junior year, I no longer felt like a stranger on the campus, learning the ropes. I felt that I *belonged* at Notre Dame.

I belonged academically. I understood the rhythm and the routines of the university and knew how to manage my energy and effort. More important, I belonged intellectually. I had learned to read for depth and insight. I had learned how to learn, and I was on fire with excitement over ideas and for the teachers who inspired them in me. I began to see connections between the things I was learning in the classroom and events of all kinds that were transpiring in the "real world".

It didn't hurt that I had broken through socially and had girlfriends. One young woman, a sophomore at St. Mary's College when I was a junior, I dated for virtually the entire year and ended up proposing to. She rejected me, thank God. I really was not ready for that responsibility.

It also didn't hurt that Notre Dame by then had a critical mass of black students, who were changing the complexion of the student body and demonstrating the diversity of attitudes, experiences, and economic classes among black Americans.

My learning seemed to come all in a rush of insights and epiphanies, some the result of design and some by happenstance.

The key to everything was my professors. I learned to identify those whose interests and teaching styles matched my interests and learning style. Follow the great teacher, I realized, and you'll learn something useful and valuable, even if it wasn't what you had in mind at the start.

Walter Nicgorski continued to be my principal mentor and patron. I took a one-on-one course from him on the Constitution, the Declaration of Independence and other documents relating to the American founding. I took two courses in political philosophy from Edward Goerner, becoming, in the process, an admirer of his cool, cerebral style of pedagogy. All of these courses provided me with foundational knowledge that I called upon almost every day of my working life.

I learned that both Goerner and Nicgorski had earned their doctorates at the University of Chicago, about which I previously had known nothing, but which I immediately began to consider as a potential next academic stop for myself. At that point, I simply assumed that I would continue in school after my undergraduate education was complete.

James W. Silver was a historian and a refugee from Mississippi. He had been for years a faculty member at the University of Mississippi, a leading historian of the South and a white advocate of racial moderation in that most benightedly racist state. In 1964, Silver published a book, "Mississippi: The Closed Society," in which he described the racist regime of terror there. Then he was run out of the state.

Doing as he had with scholars from Eastern Europe, the Communist bloc and elsewhere, Notre Dame's president, the Rev. Theodore Hesburgh, reached out to Silver and invited him to come to Notre Dame. Silver accepted and stayed in South Bend for four years, from 1965 to 1969. I took two courses from him, both on aspects of Southern history and race relations, albeit from the perspective of a Southern white man.

Silver's courses were as close as I could come to black history in those days, because Notre Dame offered no such courses. In fact, Notre Dame then had only two black faculty members. One of them, Adam Arnold, taught in the college of business, and the other, William Richardson, taught Spanish in the modern languages department.

John Dunne was a Holy Cross priest and a theologian. His courses were exercises in watching a great soul think aloud about God, man and the relationship between them. I took two of them.

And then there was Frank O'Malley. A white-haired, chainsmoking New Englander, O'Malley was one of Notre Dame's "bachelor dons". He lived in a dormitory, Lyons Hall, and taught English. Actually, O'Malley embraced English. To listen to one of his lectures—I took his course on Modern Catholic Writers—was to listen to a man in love with the language and the concepts and realities it expressed. One of the great honors of my undergraduate years was the evening O'Malley invited me to have dinner with him in the dining room at the Morris Inn, the on-campus hotel. I don't recall much of the conversation, so overcome was I with awe at breaking bread with one of Notre Dame's greatest teachers.

I still have Frank's reading list from that course, but I must admit that when I hit age sixty, I stopped promising myself I was going to read all the books on it.

I took an American History course from Marshall Smelser that proved invaluable to me throughout my working life as a journalist. I never took a course from Father James Burtchaell, a Holy Cross priest and a theologian who later became Notre Dame's first provost, but a talk he gave in my dorm one night helped me break free of my puerile understanding of Catholicism and appreciate the primacy of individual conscience. Father Charles Sheedy, another New Englander, taught me with a wry, offhanded remark one day the importance of *not* being in awe of people who could talk long and loud and seemingly learnedly, but of listening instead for good, common sense. And Father David Burrell, another Holy Cross priest who lived on the second floor of Farley, became a wise and valued friend and confessor.

In many ways, I was terribly, painfully naïve. I grew up in a household where education was respected, and these men—these intellectuals—I not only revered but reverenced. It didn't take much time out in the real world for me to discover that intellect is not the same thing as wisdom, and that reverence ought to be bestowed only on the divine. But these teachers awakened and nurtured something in me that was magical. I mean no disrespect to any other individual or institution, but I wonder how anything other than tutelage through intimate, personal contact with living teachers can fairly be called "education".

Beyond the classroom, I continued to work with the Committee on Negro Enrollment. That involvement led to one of my greatest friendships and one of my greatest regrets.

The friendship was with a young assistant director of admissions named John Goldrick. A member of the Notre Dame class of 1962, John had come to Notre Dame from Hamilton, Ohio. After earning his bachelor's degree in history, he joined the Peace Corps and served two years in Thailand, where he met his future wife, Jackie Dunne, who was also a Peace Corps volunteer from Bozeman, Montana.

After the Peace Corps, Goldrick returned to Notre Dame and went to work in admissions, where recruiting minority students was part of his portfolio. I began working part-time in the admissions office and became friends with him. By the time I graduated in 1969, we had become such good friends that he asked me to be in his and Jackie's wedding, which was held in the old Log Chapel next to St. Mary's Lake on the Notre Dame campus. We have remained friends ever since. John and Jackie honored me by asking me to be godfather to their older daughter, Shaheen. When my parents came for my graduation from Notre Dame, John and Jackie hosted them for dinner at their home.

The regret had to do with my brother Christopher, whom to this day I consider one of the brightest persons I've ever known. Chris was a senior at St. Anthony High School in Washington, D.C., when I was a junior at Notre Dame. He was exactly the type of candidate every selective college would want to attract, and they all went after him.

Chris had his heart set on Harvard, and he won admission there and scholarships that would have allowed him to go for free. But I was lobbying for Notre Dame, as were Mother and Daddy, and in the end, Chris succumbed to the family pressure and "chose" Notre Dame.

A few weeks after classes started in the fall of 1968, Father Jim Burtchaell waved me down on campus one day and told me Chris was not showing up at his classes. By the end of the first semester, Chris was out.

Soon, he was drafted into the Army, did a tour of duty in Germany, and then returned to the Houston area. Then he enrolled at St. John's College in Santa Fe, one of the Great Books colleges. He found his way into the computer and IT industry and made a career. He also found a wife, to whom he has been married for more than forty years, and with whom he has raised three children who are my beloved nieces and nephew. Chris is my best friend.

In 1964, President Lyndon Johnson declared his "war on poverty," an audacious effort to rectify old inequities and open doors of opportunity for the millions of Americans, both white and black, who lived stunted lives because of economic disadvantage.

One facet of that effort was Upward Bound, a summertime educational enrichment program for low-income high school students. Notre Dame inaugurated its program in the summer of 1966, and I, a rising sophomore, was lucky enough to be hired as a counselor, along with about a dozen others, all upperclassmen.

John Kromkowski was assistant director of the program that year. John was a Notre Dame graduate and a native of South Bend. His father was a big wheel in the St. Joseph County Democratic Party. John was a graduate student in political science, working toward his doctorate. He and his wife, Nancy Germano, had four young sons, and they became like another family to me.

By the time I became a senior, John was the director of Upward Bound, and he hired me as an assistant. He also introduced me to *Cross Currents*, a quarterly publication on Catholic theology and politics that I read for many years until, as I recall, it went out of business.

In my senior year, I became an officer in the Notre Dame student government. J. Richard Rossie, a Mississippian, was elected student body president and appointed me to his cabinet as "human affairs commissioner." That was, in those days, the token slot for the black member of the cabinet, just as secretary of Health, Education and Welfare, and later secretary of Housing and Urban Development, became the token cabinet position in Washington, until President Jimmy Carter broke the mold.

Not too long into the 1968-69 academic year, someone initiated a drive to impeach Rossie. I don't recall the reason, but it probably was something that, in the large scheme of things, was not very significant but was inflated to impeachment-worthy status. (So much of what happened in student politics was more about being clever than about being wise.)

Anyway, Rossie was impeached and was forced to run again for the office he had won only the previous spring. At the same time, the budding black student organization, the Afro-American Society, was looking to flex its muscles. It decided to run a candidate against Rossie. Because I possessed something of a profile on campus, I was chosen as the society's candidate.

I had no real desire to be student body president. But I did want to "represent" for the Afro-American Society. So I ran. And I lost. And that was okay. We had served notice of our presence on campus, and that had been the point.

We demonstrated our presence in other ways as well: protesting during a speech by the arch-segregationist (and closet "miscegenationist") Senator Strom Thurmond of South Carolina; rushing onto the sacred turf of Notre Dame Stadium during halftime of a game against Georgia Tech with banners calling for the university to recruit more black players; and mounting a black literary festival to expose ourselves and the rest of the campus to such figures as Ralph Ellison and Haki Madhubuti (then Don L. Lee).

Amid all this and with the advice and encouragement of my faculty mentors, I was pursuing opportunities for my next step after graduation. I applied for fellowships and admission to several graduate programs in political science. This, even though I knew that my student deferment would end after graduation, and I might be drafted for military service.

Vietnam and the war there was a constant, brooding presence in our minds then, hovering over everything we did. Lyndon Johnson had been driven out of the Democratic presidential race in March 1968 by Sen. Eugene McCarthy and the anti-war forces in the party. But the war still ground on, consuming more lives—American and Vietnamese—and ruining trust among the American people in the wisdom and honesty of their leaders.

In the end, I ended up being designated a Woodrow Wilson Fellow and gaining admission to the University of Chicago.

The idea of Chicago excited me. It had since my high school days in Terre Haute, when I used to listen to grainy, staticky broadcasts of music and news from there on 50,000-watt AM radio stations. We had some relatives there, cousins of Mother and Daddy from Texas and Louisiana. I didn't know them well, but I thought they must live glamorous lives in the big city. Now, at last, I would be going there.

My last semester at Notre Dame was a golden time. I was living in a fourth-floor room in Farley with another black student, Ted Jones. Ted was a junior. He had come to Notre Dame as a football player, a graduate of Houston's legendary Wheatley High School, where he had been coached by another cousin of my dad, Frank Walker.

At some point, Ted quit football and turned his attention to student government. He was good at it—smart, sociable and silver-tongued. He made a bid to become vice president of the student body, but he and the fellow at the top of the ticket went down to defeat.

I had also become friends with another younger black student, a fellow from Pittsburgh named David Krashna. David was a sophomore and, while quieter and more reserved than Ted, was also politically ambitious. In spring 1970, the year after I graduated, David ran for and won the student body presidency.

We used to hang out in the evening in Ted's and my room, joined by friends from various quarters of the campus, including a young woman from St. Mary's whom I was dating. We would play wild games of bid whist, smoke cigarettes, drink a little alcohol, debate the issues of the day, and revel in each other's company. All of this against a musical backdrop of Motown artists like the Supremes and the Temptations, Isaac Hayes, and even a country artist who was a favorite of Ted's, Joe South. We must have worn the grooves out of one particular record, Nina Simone's *Nuff Said*.

What, I ask myself as I think back on those days, did we do to deserve such privilege? More important, have I done enough since then to *earn* that privilege and pay it forward?

He couldn't have had us in mind, but the great Bob Dylan wrote a song that perfectly evokes those days and my feelings about them. It's called "Bob Dylan's Dream". It is an older man's reminiscence about a group of friends, not unlike ours, who during their youth gathered in cheerful conviviality. But later, inevitably, each went his or her own way.

Dylan concludes:

"Now many a year has passed and gone,
Many a gamble has been lost and won
And many a road taken by many a first friend
And each one I've never seen again.

"I wish, I wish, I wish in vain
That we could sit simply in that room again
Ten thousand dollars at the drop of a hat
I'd give it all gladly if our lives could be like that."

BEFORE THE BYLINE DON WYCLIFF

CHAPTER 12
FINDING MY CALLING

I arrived on the University of Chicago campus in mid-September 1969. I knew right away that I had made a mistake. It was the first of a few times in my life that I arrived at a place I had sought to be, only to realize immediately that I didn't belong there.

I didn't belong at the U. of C. I didn't belong in school at all. Since the age of six, I had done nothing but go to school, and I was tired of it. I wanted to be out in the world, creating change. I wanted to see up close and be involved in the sound and fury and social turbulence of the time. I wanted to be in the struggle for civil rights and black advancement. I wanted to be among those pressing for an end to the senseless, ceaseless war in Vietnam, which ground on mercilessly year after year.

Instead, I was in school again for the seventeenth straight year, doing the only thing I had ever done, the only thing I really knew how to do: go to school. I was going along with the program. I knew that if I kept at it, I would receive a prestigious doctorate and find a job teaching political science at a college somewhere.

More school.

Or maybe I would go nuts and find myself in a hospital somewhere. Often during my time in Hyde Park, I strode around the campus with its gray buildings under the gray winter skies of Chicago and thought that I could not endure another moment of that existence.

The problem was that while I knew I didn't want to be in grad school, I didn't know where I *did* want to be.

Although hardly desired, Vietnam was a possible alternative. With the completion of my degree at Notre Dame, my student deferment had run out, and I was now eligible to be drafted. A more equitable draft lottery was working its way toward implementation in Washington, however, so there was hope I might never be.

I was uncomfortable with Chicago, the city I had longed to experience. It was the biggest city I had ever lived in and a place radically different from pastoral, peaceful Notre Dame. I love Chicago now, but back then, it seemed overwhelming: the people so numerous, the pace so fast and relentless, the complexity so daunting.

I recall finding myself at one point with no cash and needing to cash a check. But I couldn't find a place to do it. And once again, I got that sense of financial precariousness that I had felt when my family moved from Dayton to Ashland. There was no one to whom I could say in a pinch, "Charge it."

Graduate study is, by its very nature, an isolating, solitary business. Everybody works on his or her own projects and ideas. But that sense of isolation was heightened at this university, among all those extremely cerebral people, behind those gray walls under perpetually gray Midwestern winter skies. It was a virtual prescription for depression, and I suspect if I hadn't walked away when I finally did, they'd have had to carry me away one day on a gurney.

Part of my problem was money. I had a fellowship that provided me enough money to pay my rent of $75 per month and buy food. But there was no excess for anything more.

And my apartment was not in tony, relatively safe Hyde Park, where the university is situated and most of my colleagues lived, but several blocks north, at 47th Street and Drexel Boulevard, true ghetto. Friends would be startled when I told them where I lived. They were even more startled when I told them I routinely walked or bicycled back and forth between the campus and home. Fear of crime was rife at the time. And not without reason. During my time at the U. of C., a student was shot to death on a Hyde Park street in an attempted robbery.

I had my own small brush with criminal violence one night at home. I was working in my third-floor apartment when I heard a racket from the hallway outside. I opened my door and looked down the stairwell to the first-floor entryway, where I saw a fellow trying to pry my bike loose from the pillar to which I routinely chained it. "Hey!" I shouted. "Leave that bike alone!" He looked up at me, grinned and, as I watched, pulled out a knife and slashed both of my tires. Only later did it cross my mind that it was fortunate I hadn't rushed down to physically confront him.

To supplement my fellowship income, I signed up to work as a substitute teacher in the Chicago Public Schools. The CPS always needed subs. The drill was that you would call a certain number very early on any day you were available to work, and they would call you a short time later with an assignment. Over the period I was there, I subbed at about half a dozen South Side elementary schools. At one of them—I don't remember which—the principal offered me a position as the school's permanent sub. I declined.

I did not enjoy the substitute experience, but it did give me some insight into the problems that children and their teachers encountered in those inner-city schools. I witnessed the deleterious effects of poverty on kids. And I saw how one child with behavioral problems can disrupt a whole classroom and keep others from learning.

The start of my enrollment at the university coincided with the beginning, on September 24, 1969, of the infamous federal trial of the Chicago Eight, who eventually became the Chicago Seven. The Eight were an assortment of antiwar activists who had been involved in street protests during the 1968 Democratic National Convention. They included Abbie Hoffman, Jerry Rubin, Rennie Davis, David Dellinger, John Froines, Tom Hayden, Lee Weiner, and Bobby Seale. They were accused of conspiring to cross state lines to incite violence at the convention.

Seale, a co-founder and national minister of defense of the Black Panther Party, was the only one of the Eight I knew anything about. The Panthers had burst into the national consciousness in May of 1967, when a group of them, exercising their rights under California law, showed up at a hearing at the state capitol in Sacramento carrying loaded weapons. With their black berets, black leather jackets, big Afros and serious, unsmiling visages, they cut a radically different figure than the suit-and-tie wearing traditional civil rights leaders. And their philosophy of black self-defense was a sharp ideological counterpoint to the nonviolent direct action approach of Dr. King and others.

The trial of the Eight was a national news story and a regular topic of concern and conversation among students on campus. The proceeding oscillated between farce and tragedy, with Abbie Hoffman and Rubin baiting Judge Julius Hoffmann (no relation to Abbie) with a variety of antics, while Seale, the odd man out in the alleged conspiracy, protested rulings that kept him from being represented by the attorney of his choice.

Ultimately, Seale so provoked the old judge that Hoffman had him bound, gagged, and chained to a chair in the courtroom. Finally, the judge declared a mistrial in his case, reducing the Eight to Seven. All were acquitted of the conspiracy charge, but some were convicted of other offenses. In the end, all the convictions were overturned on appeal, and the government decided not to try them again.

As for my actual academic work, I gravitated toward courses in political philosophy, as I had as an undergrad. I took Joseph Cropsey's courses on the political philosophies of Thomas Aquinas and Thomas

Hobbes. I took a seminar course at the law school with three of the university's stars: Gerhard Casper, law professor who later became president of Stanford University; Edward Shils, sociologist; and Harry Kalven, an eminence of legal scholarship.

I became friends with three other black graduate students in political science, Dianne Pinderhughes, Lorenzo Morris, and Charles Henry. All three went on to have distinguished careers in the field: Henry at the University of California at Berkeley, Morris at Howard University, and Pinderhughes at the University of Illinois at Champaign-Urbana and, later, Notre Dame. Dianne has done me the honor of asking me to speak to her classes from time to time. And we regularly see each other at Sunday Mass at St. Augustine Catholic Church on the west side of South Bend.

I developed more friendships that would be important later in my life. Tom Vitullo, who as a Notre Dame undergraduate had been a protégé of Edward Goerner, and his wife, Julia Vitullo-Martin, were both at Chicago then.

* * *

December 4, 1969, marked the beginning of the end of my graduate school experience. My alarm went off at 7 a.m. I reached out from beneath the covers on my bed and turned on my radio. It was tuned to the local all-news station, WBBM-AM. Within seconds, I heard the news: A Chicago police unit, detailed to the office of Cook County State's Attorney Edward V. Hanrahan, had raided the West Side headquarters of the Illinois Black Panther Party during the night. Two members of the Panthers had been killed in what the police described as a shootout: Fred Hampton, the party chairman, and Mark Clark, a rank-and-file member from downstate Illinois.

The news hit me like a lightning bolt out of a clear blue sky: Fred Hampton was dead.

BEFORE THE BYLINE DON WYCLIFF

I had never met Hampton. I knew about him only because of what I had read in the newspapers and seen on television. One of those reports—a television interview he gave not long before his death—impressed me. Hampton struck me as highly intelligent and passionately concerned about his people, our people, black people. There was a depth to him that belied the popular characterizations of him as a mere rabble-rouser or gangster. He was a man I had wanted to hear more of and from.

And now he was dead.

In the days and weeks after the police raid, I followed news coverage of the killings obsessively. Chicago then had five daily newspapers—four mainstream publications and one, the *Chicago Defender*, targeted to the black audience. I made it my business to read every word in each of them about the Panther "shootout." Television was not as readily accessible to me then as newspapers were, but I watched as much news coverage as I could, including a police "reenactment" of the raid broadcast on WBBM TV.

It gradually became evident that there had been no shootout at all. Rather, it was a shoot-in by the police, an assassination. The clincher was the close-up front-page photo in the December 12 editions of the *Chicago Sun-Times* showing rusted nail heads in the door of the Panthers' apartment. The *Chicago Tribune* had earlier published a photo purporting to show bullet holes in the door created by gunfire from within. "Those 'bullet holes' aren't" read the headline in the *Sun-Times*, giving the lie to the police claim that the Panthers had fired at them.

At some point, it occurred to me that the people putting out these news reports were performing an enormous public service. Newspapers had been part of my daily life since I began devouring the comics in the *Ashland Daily Independent* in the mid-1950s. I could recall watching television news as far back as John Cameron Swayze's Camel News

Caravan, also in the 1950s. Chet Huntley and David Brinkley on NBC and Walter Cronkite on CBS were daily presences in our home in the 1960s. And one of my most enduring memories was of CBS News's Roger Mudd broadcasting daily from the U.S. Capitol on the progress of the Civil Rights Act of 1964 as it moved toward passage by Congress.

But before the killing of Fred Hampton, I had never reflected on journalism's purposes and methods. It had always just been there, a product available if you wanted it. And I had never imagined that I could do journalism. I had had no training, and I didn't know anyone who worked in the field.

But I admired what these Chicago journalists were doing and decided I wanted to do it also. I liked that they asked tough questions of people in authority, the kind of questions I wanted to ask. I knew I could write decently and ask intelligent questions, and figure things out. So how hard could it be? I figured I could learn what I needed to if I could find the right opportunity.

I reflect on all this now and am astonished at my temerity. But one of the benefits of youth is not knowing what you cannot do. So you'll try anything.

I enrolled for the second quarter of the academic year at the U. of C., but already I was thinking of when and how I might make the jump from academia to journalism. I decided I would finish the quarter, leave the university, and go home to Texas. By this time, Mother and Daddy and my five youngest siblings were living in Texarkana, where Daddy had been most recently transferred. But "home" remained Dayton, and Grandma's house on the hillside. I called her and asked whether I could live with her and Aunt Willie while I looked for a job. She eagerly said yes.

Toward the end of March, I obtained a driveaway—a car I contracted to drive to Houston for its owner—loaded up my meager be-

BEFORE THE BYLINE DON WYCLIFF

longings, and left Chicago. Most of what I owned were books, and my friends John and Jackie Goldrick allowed me to store them in their garage in South Bend. Then I drove south to Texas.

Grandma and Aunt Willie welcomed me, sheltered me, and fed me. And when I was ready to start job-hunting, Grandma let me use her Chevy Nova to make the rounds of potential employers in Houston.

Only much later did I appreciate the irony in my situation. I had returned to Texas to try to make a career two decades after my father left the state in frustration at being unable to find a decently remunerative job. Thanks to the revolution wrought by Lyndon Johnson, Martin Luther King Jr. and the Civil Rights Movement, I had come of age in a new Texas, a new America.

I went first to KHOU-TV, the CBS affiliate in Houston. I went unannounced, carrying a copy of my meager resume and clippings of a couple of articles I had written for the Notre Dame student magazine, *The Scholastic*. I told the receptionist I was looking for a job as a news reporter and asked to speak to the station manager. She made a call, and a few minutes later, a gentleman came out and greeted me. He was the station's news director. He looked at my resume and listened to my pitch. Then, very politely, he told me he had no openings on his staff, but he wished me well in my job search. We shook hands and parted.

My next stop was *The Houston Post*, one of the city's two major newspapers. I had looked up the paper's address in a directory at a library and went to that downtown address. It turned out, however, that the *Post* had recently moved to a beautiful new building southwest of downtown, just off a freeway leading toward Victoria, Texas.

I drove there and presented myself, unannounced, at a reception desk. I said I wanted to apply for a job as a reporter. The lady at the desk sent me to the human resources department, where another lady listened to my request and gave me an application to fill out.

When I finished the application, she studied it for several minutes and then asked me to have a seat. She disappeared for a while and, when she came back, asked me to accompany her to the editorial department. There she introduced me to the newspaper's managing editor, O.D. Wilson.

Wilson welcomed me into his office and we chatted for about 10 minutes. He asked me about my background, my education, and my writing experience. He was particularly interested in my Notre Dame connection and was surprised to learn that I hailed from Dayton, so close by. At the end of the conversation, he asked me to come back next week.

I didn't know at the time that the *Post* had only one black reporter, a fellow named Robert C. Newberry, who would become a friend and mentor. I did know that Houston, like many other cities, had a black population that was pressing for political power and economic and social advancement. Ironically, one of those pressing hardest was a young man named Carl Hampton (no relation to Fred), who headed a Black Panther-type organization called Peoples Party II.

When I returned to Wilson's office the next week, he gave me a writing test: basic grammar, spelling, punctuation, and syntax. Then he introduced me to his boss, Edwin Hunter, the editor of the paper, and together they laid out a proposal: They would bring me onto the staff as a reporter trainee. I'd work first on Action Line, a reader advocacy column that responded to consumer complaints and dilemmas. That would require me to dig into reference works, phone directories, the newspaper's morgue and other resources and call people on the telephone for information.

After a stint on Action Line, I would be placed under the tutelage of a former city editor of the newspaper, C.W. Skipper, who would teach me how to recognize a news story and how to think and behave like a reporter. If I progressed appropriately in those two situations, I would be given the chance to work on a suburban news beat, accompanying a seasoned reporter.

As Hunter and Wilson talked, there was no question in my mind that I would accept the proposal. This was the chance I had been hoping for. This was where that long and winding road—from Dayton to Ashland to Denver to Terre Haute to Notre Dame to Chicago—had brought me. Not to the end of a journey, but to a new commencement, to the starting line of a forty-year effort to make a difference in the world through facts and the written word. It had brought me to the launch pad of my career.

A few days later, I reported to the newspaper to begin work. To begin a life's work.

EPILOGUE

The most satisfying moment of my newspaper career happened almost at the end of it. It was 2003, and I was serving as public editor, or ombudsman, of the *Chicago Tribune*. I wrote a column in which I took the U.S. government to task for its treatment of Muhammad Salah, a Palestinian American man who lived with his family in the suburb of Broadview, Illinois.

Salah had been subjected to almost a decade of piñata-like treatment, first by the Israeli government and then by the U.S. Arrested in 1993 during a trip to his homeland, he underwent fifty-five days of interrogation by the Israeli military and then spent almost five years in a military prison after allegedly admitting that he had provided funding to Hamas.

While he was imprisoned, the U.S. government piled on by labelling him a "specially designated terrorist," a unique tag that forbade him to conduct any kind of normal financial transaction—get a job, pay his rent, get medical care—without a special license from the government. In other words, Salah was being punished without having been charged, tried and found guilty by a jury of his peers, as the U.S. Constitution requires.

If the government had the goods on Salah, I wrote, let it charge

BEFORE THE BYLINE DON WYCLIFF

him, try him and abide by the judicially determined result. Otherwise, call off the dogs.

Eventually—three years later—the government did just that. Salah was tried along with another man for allegedly conspiring to support Hamas extremists and for obstructing justice by lying in a civil lawsuit filed by the family of a victim of terrorism. He was acquitted on the first charge and convicted of the second.

Salah's wife told me later, "You were the first person of any prominence to speak up for us."

My prominence was minimal but apparently sufficient to offer some succor to a man and his family who, I felt, were being subjected by their government—and *mine*—to treatment that was fundamentally un-American. That expression of gratitude meant more to me than any prize I might have won.

I grew up a believer in America. Back in my childhood, when television stations still "signed off" at the end of their broadcast days, my siblings and I would stand stiffly at attention and salute as the image of a fluttering American flag filled the screen and the national anthem played.

When I had to memorize the Declaration of Independence, the Gettysburg Address, or the preamble to the U.S. Constitution, I took seriously all those high-minded ideals and principles. Especially this one:

"We hold these truths to be self-evident, that all men are created equal and that they are endowed by their creator with certain unalienable rights, that among these are life, liberty and the pursuit of happiness."

And when I got older and studied the Constitution and the Bill of Rights, I believed those clauses about freedom of religion, speech, press, assembly and petition. And I thought the document really meant it when it said "No person shall be...deprived of life, liberty, or property, without due process of law...".

It was the violation of that principle that so deeply aggrieved me when I heard on December 4, 1969, that Fred Hampton had been killed. I felt that same sense of grievance about Muhammad Salah, and every day he remained under sanction by the Treasury Department was a fresh offense to my sense of what America is supposed to be and do.

My days in the journalistic trenches are over. But America has lately taken a turn that suggests violations of due process, free speech, voting rights and all the other principles enshrined in our sacred documents will be abundant in the days and years to come. There will be no shortage of work for new generations of young journalists.

BEFORE THE BYLINE DON WYCLIFF

ACKNOWLEDGMENTS

I could not have produced this book of memories without the help and generous cooperation of my seven surviving sisters and brothers: Karen, Chris, Ida, Joy, Judith, Jean, and Brian.

My wife Pamela was a constant source of encouragement, as was the congregation of Pam's church, the Unitarian Universalist Fellowship of Elkhart (Indiana), who allowed me to read parts of the manuscript to them on three different occasions.

My former Chicago Tribune colleague Dawn Turner generously shared her knowledge of the writing and publishing process.

And my sons, Matthew and Grant, gave me the motivation to tell this story of the Wycliff family at a special moment in American history.

www.ingramcontent.com/pod-product-compliance
Lightning Source LLC
Chambersburg PA
CBHW050525100526
44581CB00007B/128/J